96 Quick Breads: Delicious Recipes for Every Occasion

Spice Square Kami

Contents

4

INTRODUCTION

Welcome to Cookbook 96 Quick Breads: Delicious Recipes for Every Occasion! This book has been designed to provide quick and easy recipes for delicious homemade breads perfect for any occasion. This book is perfect for those who have never baked before, or those with a wealth of experience in the kitchen.

When it comes to simple, scrumptious and fast bread recipes, look no further than Cookbook 96 Quick Breads: Delicious Recipes for Every Occasion! From classic sweet loaves to rich and savory herb focaccia to nutty maple nutloaf, each recipe will provide a tasty mouthwatering result.

This book simplifies the art of bread-baking with time-saving recipes that come together easily. You will learn the basics of bread-making from the ground up, from how to properly measure ingredients to how to knead and shape your dough. Bake times and temperatures are clearly marked for each recipe, so that you can replicate professional-style results in your own kitchen.

If you're looking for a quick meal, Cookbook 96 Quick Breads offers a range of delicious ideas from cheese-stuffed buns to crispy ciabatta. And if you'd rather explore some lighter and sweeter options, try a moist banana-apple loaf or a fresh blueberry muffin. Quick breads are a great way to show your creative culinary side—try adding some unique ingredients such as chocolate chips, walnuts or dried fruits.

All of the recipes inside Cookbook 96 Quick Breads are easy to make and can be adapted to your individual taste. You'll find something perfect to enjoy again and again, with evocative flavor combinations, delightful textures and eye-catching presentation. So take this adventure with us into the world of quick breads and discover all the possibilities that await. Enjoy!

1. Apple Cinnamon Quick Bread

This Apple Cinnamon Quick Bread is an easy fall recipe that can be enjoyed as a breakfast or dessert treat! It is flavorful, moist, and delicious and comes together with minimal effort.

Serving: This recipe yields 1 loaf | Preparation Time: 10 minutes | Ready Time: 45 minutes

Ingredients:
- 2 cups all-purpose flour
- 1 cup white sugar
- 2 teaspoons baking powder
- 2 teaspoons ground cinnamon
- 1/4 teaspoon salt
- 1/4 teaspoon baking soda
- 1 egg
- 1/2 cup butter, melted
- 1 teaspoon vanilla extract
- 1 cup diced apples
- 1 teaspoon lemon juice

Instructions:
1. Preheat the oven to 350 degrees F. Grease a 9x5 inch loaf pan.
2. In a large bowl, whisk together the flour, sugar, baking powder, cinnamon, salt, and baking soda.
3. In a separate bowl, mix the egg, melted butter, and vanilla extract together until combined.
4. Add the wet ingredients to the dry ingredients and mix until combined.
5. Add the diced apples and lemon juice to the mixture and fold in until evenly distributed.
6. Pour the batter into the prepared loaf pan and bake for 40-45 minutes or until a tester comes out of the center clean.
7. Allow to cool before cutting and serving. Enjoy!

Nutrition Information:
Calories: 272, Fat: 11g, Saturated Fat: 6g, Cholesterol: 44mg, Sodium: 148mg, Potassium: 123mg, Carbohydrates: 39g, Fiber: 1g, Sugar: 19g, Protein: 4g

2. Banana Bread

Banana Bread is a moist and delicious quick bread made with overripe bananas, sugar, butter and other basic ingredients. It is sweet enough to be dessert and versatile enough to be enjoyed as a snack or even breakfast.

Serving: Makes 1 loaf | Preparation Time: 15 minutes | Ready Time: 1 hour and 10 minutes.

Ingredients:
- 2 cups all-purpose flour
- 1 teaspoon baking soda
- 1 teaspoon salt
- 1/2 cup (1 stick) butter, melted
- 3/4 cup white sugar
- 2 eggs, lightly beaten
- 2 ripe bananas, mashed
- 1/4 cup buttermilk (or substitute plain Greek yogurt)
- 1 teaspoon vanilla extract

Instructions:
1. Preheat the oven to 350F. Grease a 9x5 inch loaf pan.
2. In a large bowl, whisk together the flour, baking soda and salt.
3. In a separate bowl, cream together the butter and sugar. Then add the eggs, mashed banana, buttermilk (or yogurt) and vanilla extract, mixing until just incorporated.
4. Pour the wet ingredients into the dry ingredients, stirring until just combined.
5. Spoon the batter into the prepared pan, smoothing the top. Bake for 45 minutes.
6. Reduce the oven temperature to 325F and bake for an additional 20 minutes or until a toothpick inserted into the center comes out clean.
7. Allow the loaf to cool in the pan before turning out onto a wire rack to cool completely.

Nutrition Information:

Serving size: 1 slice (1/12 of loaf)
Calories: 182, Fat: 7g, Saturated Fat: 4g, Cholesterol: 43mg, Sodium: 298mg, Carbohydrates: 27g, Fiber: 1g, Sugar: 13g, Protein: 3g

3. Blueberry Cornmeal Quick Bread

Blueberry Cornmeal Quick Bread is a simple and delicious summertime recipe perfect for a breakfast, brunch, or snack. This delicious bread is made with fluffy buttermilk and sweet blueberries, and it only takes 40 minutes to prepare and bake.

Serving: This quick bread can make 9 slices | Preparation Time: 10 minutes | Ready Time: 30 minutes

Ingredients:
- 2 cups all-purpose flour
- 1 cup yellow cornmeal
- 1 teaspoon baking soda
- 2 teaspoons baking powder
- 1 teaspoon salt
- 1/2 cup (1 stick) butter, at room temperature
- 1 cup sugar
- 2 large eggs
- 1 cup buttermilk
- 1 teaspoon vanilla extract
- 1 1/2 cups fresh or frozen blueberries

Instructions:
1. Preheat oven to 350F. Grease a 9x5-inch loaf pan.
2. In a medium bowl, combine flour, cornmeal, baking soda, baking powder, and salt. Set aside.
3. In a large bowl, cream together butter and sugar until light and fluffy. Add eggs one at a time, beating well after each addition. Beat in buttermilk and vanilla extract.
4. Gradually add dry ingredients to wet ingredients and mix until combined. Stir in blueberries.

5. Pour batter into prepared loaf pan and spread evenly. Bake for 30-35 minutes or until a toothpick inserted into the center comes out clean. Let cool before slicing.

Nutrition Information:
Per 1 slice: 220 Calories, 11g Fat, 28g Carbohydrates, 4g Protein.

4. Sour Cream Date-Nut Bread

Sour Cream Date-Nut Bread is an irresistibly delicious and moist bread that combines sweet dates and crunchy nuts in a delightful way. It makes for a great dessert, snack or breakfast side.

Serving: 10-12 | Preparation Time: 15 minutes | Ready Time: 1 hour 30 minutes

Ingredients:
- 2 cups all-purpose flour
- 1 teaspoon baking soda
- 1 teaspoon baking powder
- 1/2 teaspoon ground cinnamon
- 1/2 cup butter
- 1 cup packed brown sugar
- 2 eggs
- 1 teaspoon vanilla extract
- 1 cup sour cream
- 1 1/2 cups pitted chopped dates
- 1/2 cup coarsely chopped walnuts

Instructions:
1. Preheat the oven to 350F (175°C). Grease an 8x4 inch (20x10 cm) loaf pan.
2. In a medium bowl, combine the flour, baking soda, baking powder, and ground cinnamon.
3. In a large bowl, cream together the butter and brown sugar. Beat in the eggs, one at a time, until light and fluffy. Stir in the vanilla extract.
4. Stir the dry ingredients into the batter alternately with the sour cream. Mix in the dates and walnuts.

5. Pour the batter into the prepared loaf pan.

6. Bake for 55 minutes to 65 minutes in the preheated oven, or until a toothpick inserted into the center of the loaf comes out clean.

7. Let cool in the pan for 10 minutes, then turn out onto a wire rack and cool.

Nutrition Information:

Serving size: 1 slice (approx. 1/12 of a loaf), Calories: 200 kcal, Fat: 8 g, Carbohydrates: 27 g, Protein: 4 g, Sodium: 100 mg, Cholesterol: 30 mg

5. Zucchini Bread

Zucchini Bread is a delicious and healthy snack or breakfast option, made with grated zucchini, nuts, and spices. It has a light texture and sweet, nutty flavor that's perfect for any day.

Serving: Makes 1 loaf, approximately 16 slices | Preparation Time: 15 minutes | Ready Time: 1 hour, 15 minutes

Ingredients:

- 2 1/2 cups all-purpose flour
- 2 teaspoons baking powder
- 1 teaspoon baking soda
- 1 teaspoon salt
- 1 teaspoon ground cinnamon
- 1/2 teaspoon ground nutmeg
- 1/4 teaspoon ground allspice
- 2 eggs
- 1 cup granulated sugar
- 1/2 cup vegetable oil
- 1 teaspoon vanilla extract
- 2 cups grated zucchini
- 1/2 cup chopped walnuts, optional

Instructions:

1. Preheat oven to 350F. Grease a 9x5-inch loaf pan with cooking spray or butter.

2. In a medium bowl, whisk together the flour, baking powder, baking soda, salt, cinnamon, nutmeg, and allspice.
3. In a separate bowl, beat the eggs until light and fluffy. Mix in the sugar, vegetable oil, and vanilla. Gently fold in the grated zucchini.
4. Add the dry ingredients to the wet ingredients and mix just until combined. Fold in the walnuts, if using.
5. Transfer the batter to the prepared pan. Bake for 50-60 minutes, or until a toothpick inserted into the center comes out clean. Allow to cool completely before slicing.

Nutrition Information (per slice):
210 calories; 9g fat; 27g carbohydrates; 3g protein.

6. Pumpkin Bread

Pumpkin Bread is a moist and flavorful quick bread recipe. It is deliciously spiced with traditional pumpkin spices and makes a great snack or dessert.

Serving: Makes 1 loaf (approximately 10-12 slices) | Preparation Time: 20 minutes | Ready Time: 1 hour 10 minutes

Ingredients:
-11/2 cups all-purpose flour
-1 teaspoon ground cinnamon
-1/2 teaspoon ground ginger
-1/2 teaspoon freshly ground nutmeg
-1/2 teaspoon ground cloves
-1/2 teaspoon baking powder
-1/2 teaspoon baking soda
-1/2 teaspoon salt
-1 cup packed light brown sugar
-2 large eggs
-1 cup canned pumpkin puree
-1/2 cup vegetable oil
-1/2 cup raisins, chopped nuts, or dried cranberries (optional)

Instructions:

1. Preheat oven to 350F. Grease 9x5-inch loaf pan; set aside.
2. In a medium bowl, whisk together the flour, cinnamon, ginger, nutmeg, cloves, baking powder, baking soda and salt; set aside.
3. In a separate bowl, beat together the brown sugar, eggs, pumpkin puree and vegetable oil until smooth.
4. Gradually stir in the flour mixture, stirring just until mixed.
5. Fold in raisins, nuts or cranberries, if desired.
6. Pour batter into prepared pan and bake for 1 hour 10 minutes, or until a toothpick inserted in the center of the loaf comes out clean.
7. Cool in pan for ten minutes and then turn out onto a wire rack to cool completely.

Nutrition Information:
Calories: 186kcal; Carbohydrates; 26g; Protein: 3g; Fat: 8g; Saturated Fat: 5g; Trans Fat: 0g; Cholesterol: 29mg; Sodium: 147mg; Potassium: 132mg; Fiber: 1g; Sugar: 15g; Vitamin A: 1984IU; Vitamin C: 1mg; Calcium: 33mg; Iron: 1mg

7. Carrot Bread

Carrot Bread: Deliciously moist and lightly spiced with cinnamon, Carrot Bread is a scrumptious treat sure to satisfy even the pickiest snackers!

Serving: 8-10 pieces | Preparation Time: 15 minutes | Ready Time: 1 hour.

Ingredients:
- 2 cups all-purpose flour
- 1 teaspoon baking powder
- 1 teaspoon baking soda
- 1 teaspoon ground cinnamon
- 1/4 teaspoon ground nutmeg
- Pinch of salt
- 3/4 cup granulated sugar
- 2 eggs
- 2/3 cup vegetable oil
- 1 cup grated carrots
- 1/2 cup chopped walnuts

- 1/2 cup raisins

Instructions:
1. Preheat oven to 350F. Grease and flour a 9x5 inch loaf pan.
2. In a medium bowl, mix together the flour, baking powder, baking soda, cinnamon, nutmeg, and salt.
3. In a separate bowl, beat together the sugar, eggs, and oil until frothy.
4. Slowly stir the wet ingredients into the dry ingredients until just combined.
5. Fold in the carrots, walnuts, and raisins until evenly distributed.
6. Pour the batter into the greased pan and bake for 45-50 minutes until a toothpick inserted into the center comes out clean.
7. Allow to cool before slicing and serving.

Nutrition Information:
Serving size: 1/8th of loaf, Calories: 220, Fat: 11g, Carbohydrates: 29g, Protein: 3g

8. Chocolate Chip Pumpkin Bread

Chocolate Chip Pumpkin Bread is a delightful way to enjoy the flavors of pumpkin and chocolate together. This tasty bread is vegan, gluten-free, and packed with protein.

Serving: Serves 12 | Preparation Time: 10 minutes | Ready Time: 55 minutes

Ingredients:
-1/4 cup vegan butter
-1/4 cup coconut oil
-1/2 cup maple syrup
-1/2 cup coconut sugar
-1 teaspoon pure vanilla extract
-1 1/2 cups pumpkin puree
-1/2 cup almond milk
-2 cups gluten-free all-purpose flour
-1 teaspoon baking powder
-1 teaspoon baking soda

-1/2 teaspoon sea salt
-3/4 teaspoon ground cinnamon
-1/2 teaspoon ground ginger
-1/2 cup vegan chocolate chips

Instructions:
1. Preheat the oven to 350 degrees F (175 degrees C). Grease an 8x4 inch loaf pan with vegan butter.
2. In a large bowl, cream together the vegan butter and coconut oil. Beat in the maple syrup and coconut sugar until light and fluffy. Beat in the vanilla and pumpkin puree.
3. In a separate bowl, whisk together the almond milk, flour, baking powder, baking soda, sea salt, cinnamon, and ginger.
4. Gradually add the dry ingredients to the wet ingredients, stirring to combine. Fold in the chocolate chips.
5. Pour the batter into the greased loaf pan and bake for 50 to 55 minutes, or until a toothpick inserted into the center comes out clean.
6. Allow the bread to cool in the pan for 10 minutes before transferring to a wire rack to cool completely.

Nutrition Information:
Serving Size: 1 slice, Calories: 240, Total Fat: 12g, Saturated Fat: 7g, Trans Fat: 0g, Cholesterol: 0mg, Sodium: 239mg, Total Carbohydrates: 30g, Fiber: 2g, Sugars: 16g, Protein: 4g

9. Cranberry Orange Quick Bread

This zesty Cranberry Orange Quick Bread is an incredibly easy and delicious bread recipe that comes together quickly. Perfect for breakfast treats or mid-day snacks, this rich, moist quick bread will have your family begging for more!

Serving: Makes one 9x5-inch loaf | Preparation Time: 10 minutes

Ingredients
  - 2 cups all-purpose flour
  - 1 teaspoon baking powder
  - 1/4 teaspoon baking soda

16

- 1/4 teaspoon salt
- 1/2 cup (1 stick) butter, softened
- 3/4 cup granulated sugar
- 2 large eggs
- 1 cup orange juice
- Zest of one orange
- 1 teaspoon vanilla extract
- 1 1/2 cups fresh cranberries

Instructions
1. Preheat oven to 350F. Grease 9x5-inch loaf pan with butter or cooking spray; set aside.
2. In a medium bowl, whisk together the flour, baking powder, baking soda, and salt; set aside.
3. In a large bowl, beat together the butter and sugar until light and fluffy. Add the eggs, one at a time, mixing until incorporated.
4. Add the orange juice, orange zest, and vanilla extract, mixing until combined.
5. Gradually add the flour mixture until completely combined.
6. Gently fold in the cranberries, then pour the batter into the prepared loaf pan.
7. Bake for 50-55 minutes, or until a toothpick inserted into the center comes out clean. Let cool before serving.

Nutrition Information:
1 slice serving size: 230 calories, 9g fat, 37g carbohydrates, 2g protein

10. Banana Nut Bread

This delicious Banana Nut Bread is the perfect sweet treat to start off your day. It is a simple, easy to make recipe that can be enjoyed as a snack or even served as a dessert. Serve it with a little bit of butter for a transformed classic.

Serving size: 8 | Preparation Time: 15 minutes | Ready Time: 60 minutes

Ingredients:

-3 ripe bananas
-1/3 cup melted butter
-3/4 cup dark brown sugar
-1 egg
-1 teaspoon vanilla extract
-1 teaspoon baking soda
-Pinch of salt
-1 1/2 cups all-purpose flour
-1/3 cup chopped walnuts

Instructions:
1. Preheat the oven to 350F (180°C). Grease and flour a 9x5 inch loaf tin.
2. In a medium mixing bowl, mash the bananas with a fork until completely smooth.
3. Add the melted butter, sugar, egg, and vanilla extract, and stir until combined.
4. In a separate bowl, sift together the baking soda, salt, and flour.
5. Mix the dry ingredients into the wet ingredients until just combined. Do not over mix.
6. Fold in the chopped walnuts.
7. Pour the batter into the prepared loaf tin and bake for 50 to 60 minutes, or until a toothpick inserted into the center comes out clean.

Nutrition Information:
Calories: 214 kcal, Carbohydrates: 30.7g, Protein: 3.4g, Fat: 9.6g, Saturated Fat: 4.5g, Cholesterol: 29mg, Sodium: 134mg, Potassium: 173mg, Fiber: 1.8g, Sugar: 18.3g, Vitamin A: 200 IU, Vitamin C: 3.7mg, Calcium: 23mg, Iron: 0.9mg

11. Marble Bread

Marble bread is a fun way to spice up your everyday bread. This recipe is an easy way to liven up a dull sandwich or provide an added sweetness to a cheese board. With its slight sweetness, smooth chocolate flavor, and beautiful marble pattern, this bread is an eye-catching dish that's sure to be a hit with the whole family.

Serving: Makes one 2-pound loaf | Preparation Time: 1 hour

Ingredients:
-2 cups warm (110 degrees F) water
-2 tablespoons active dry yeast
-2 teaspoons brown sugar
-2 tablespoons melted butter or vegetable oil
-1 tablespoon molasses
-3 1/2–4 cups all-purpose flour
-2 teaspoons salt
-1/2 cup cocoa powder
-1 beaten egg

Instructions:
1. In a small bowl, combine water, yeast, and sugar. Mix until dissolved and let stand until foamy, about 5 minutes.
2. In a large bowl, combine butter, molasses, 3 1/2 cups of flour and salt. Mix with a wooden spoon until combined.
3. Gradually add in the yeast mixture, stirring with a wooden spoon until the dough is stiff.
4. Turn the dough onto a lightly floured work surface and knead for about 8 minutes, or until the dough is smooth and elastic.
5. Place the dough in a greased bowl, turning to coat. Cover with a kitchen towel and let rise in a warm spot until doubled, about 30 minutes.
6. Turn the risen dough onto a lightly floured work surface. Divide the dough in half and shape each half into a flattened ball.
7. To shape one ball of dough into a circular shape, roll until it's about 1/4-inch thick. Spread the 1/2 cup of cocoa powder on one-half of the dough and fold the other side over. Press lightly to seal.
8. Place the loaf on a greased baking sheet and brush with beaten egg. Cover and let rise in a warm spot until doubled, about 30 minutes.
9. Preheat oven to 375 degrees F (190 C). Bake for 35 minutes, or until lightly browned. Transfer to a wire rack to cool.

Nutrition Information:
Calories: 208; Total Fat: 3.2 g; Saturated Fat: 1.2 g; Cholesterol: 20.4 mg; Sodium: 477.3 mg; Total Carbohydrate: 40.6 g; Dietary Fiber: 2.3 g; Sugar: 1.3 g; Protein: 6.2 g.

12. Raisin Spice Bread

Raisin Spice Bread is an easy and delicious recipe that makes a great breakfast or snack. It is a sweet, lightly spiced bread, with a hint of citrus, that is packed with raisins. This comforting and flavorful bread is sure to be a hit with everyone.

Serving: 8-10 slices | Preparation Time: 15 minutes | Ready Time: 1 hour 25 minutes

Ingredients:
- 2 cups all-purpose flour
- 1/2 teaspoon baking soda
- 1/4 teaspoon baking powder
- 1/4 teaspoon salt
- 1 teaspoon ground cinnamon
- 1/2 teaspoon ground ginger
- 1/4 teaspoon ground nutmeg
- 1/4 cup orange zest
- 2 tablespoons butter, melted
- 1/4 cup vegetable oil
- 1/2 cup white sugar
- 1/2 cup light brown sugar
- 1 large egg
- 1 teaspoon vanilla extract
- 1 cup buttermilk
- 1 cup raisins

Instructions:
1. Preheat oven to 350F (175°C) and butter a 9×5-inch loaf pan.
2. In a medium bowl, whisk together the flour, baking soda, baking powder, salt, cinnamon, ginger, and nutmeg.
3. In a larger bowl, whisk together the butter, oil, white sugar, brown sugar, egg, and vanilla extract until smooth.
4. Add the buttermilk and orange zest to the wet mixture and mix until combined.

5. Gradually add the dry ingredients to the wet and mix until just combined. Do not overmix.
6. Gently fold in the raisins until combined.
7. Pour the batter into the prepared loaf pan and spread out evenly.
8. Bake in preheated oven for 45-55 minutes, or until an inserted toothpick comes out clean.
9. Allow to cool in the pan for 15 minutes before transferring to a cooling rack to cool completely.

Nutrition Information:
Calories: 206, Total Fat: 7g, Carbohydrates: 32g, Protein: 3g, Fiber: 1g, Sugar 20g

13. Applesauce Spice Bread

This Applesauce Spice Bread is a wonderful combination of sweet apples, warm spices, and a delicious moist bread. It's a great accompaniment to a cup of tea and easy to make!

Serving: 10 slices | Preparation Time: 10 minutes | Ready Time: 50 minutes

Ingredients:
- 2 cups all-purpose flour
- 1 teaspoon baking soda
- 1 teaspoon baking powder
- 1/2 teaspoon ground cinnamon
- 1/4 teaspoon ground nutmeg
- 1/2 teaspoon salt
- 1/2 cup (1 stick) unsalted butter, softened
- 1/2 cup packed light brown sugar
- 1/3 cup granulated sugar
- 2 large eggs
- 1 cup applesauce
- 1 teaspoon vanilla extract

Instructions:
1. Preheat oven to 350F

2. Grease and flour a 9x5-inch loaf pan.
3. In a medium bowl, whisk together flour, baking soda, baking powder, cinnamon, nutmeg, and salt.
4. In a large bowl, cream together butter, brown sugar, and granulated sugar until light and fluffy.
5. Beat in eggs, one at a time.
6. Mix in applesauce and vanilla extract.
7. Slowly mix in dry ingredients until combined.
8. Pour into prepared pan and bake for 40–50 minutes or until a toothpick inserted comes out clean.

Nutrition Information:
Calories: 257, Fat: 10.5g, Carbohydrates: 37.5g, Protein: 3.5g

14. Coconut Bread

Coconut Bread is a sweet and fluffy bread made from shredded coconut and flour. This delicious bread is a perfect choice for breakfast or snack.

Serving: Makes 8 slices | Preparation Time: 10 minutes | Ready Time: 30 minutes

Ingredients:
- 1 1/2 cups all-purpose flour
- 1/2 cup shredded coconut
- 1 teaspoon baking soda
- 1/2 teaspoon salt
- 2 eggs
- 1 cup sugar
- 1/3 cup vegetable oil
- 1/2 cup milk
- 1 teaspoon vanilla extract

Instructions:
1. Preheat oven to 350F. Grease an 8×4-inch loaf pan.
2. In a medium bowl, mix flour, coconut, baking soda and salt.
3. In a large bowl, mix eggs, sugar and oil. Stir in milk and vanilla extract.

4. Mix in the flour mixture until just combined.
5. Pour batter into the prepared pan. Bake for 30 minutes or until a toothpick inserted into the center comes out clean.
6. Let cool in the pan for 10 minutes then remove from pan and let cool completely on a wire rack.

Nutrition Information:
Per slice – 150 calories, 7g fat, 18g carbohydrates, 2g protein.

15. Banana Pecan Bread

Banana Pecan Bread is a traditional, sweet loaf perfect for breakfast, snacking, or dessert! This recipe will yield a pleasantly moist and nutty loaf that will please the whole family.

Serving: Makes 1 loaf, 12 - 18 slices | Preparation Time: 10 minutes | Ready Time: 1 hour

Ingredients:
- 3 ripe bananas, mashed
- 2 large eggs
- 1/3 cup melted butter
- 1/3 cup dark brown sugar
- 1 teaspoon pure vanilla extract
- 1 teaspoon ground cinnamon
- 1/2 teaspoon allspice
- 2 cups all-purpose flour
- 1 teaspoon baking soda
- 1 teaspoon baking powder
- 1/2 teaspoon kosher salt
- 1/2 cup chopped pecans

Instructions:
1. Preheat the oven to 350 degrees F (175 degrees C). Grease one 9x5-inch loaf pan.
2. In a medium bowl, use a wooden spoon to mix together the mashed bananas, eggs, melted butter, brown sugar, vanilla extract, cinnamon and all spice.

3. In a separate bowl, mix together the flour, baking soda, baking powder and salt.
4. Place the dry ingredients into the wet ingredients and stir until just combined. Do not over mix.
5. Fold in the chopped pecans.
6. Pour the batter into the prepared loaf pan, and bake for 45 - 50 minutes, or until a and inserted toothpick comes out clean.
7. Cool in pan before slicing.

Nutrition Information:
Per Serving: Calories: 230, Total Fat: 10g, Saturated Fat: 5g, Trans Fat: 0g, Unsaturated Fat: 5g, Cholesterol: 70mg, Sodium: 240mg, Carbohydrates: 32g, Fiber: 2g, Sugar: 18g, Protein: 4g

16. Lemon Poppyseed Bread

Lemon Poppyseed Bread is a delicious, zesty twist on a classic favorite. This easy to make bread has the perfect blend of sharp lemon flavor and crunchy poppyseeds that blend together for a mouthwatering treat.

Servings: 8 slices | Preparation Time: 15 minutes | Ready Time: 1 hour and 5 minutes.

Ingredients:
- 2 cups all-purpose flour
- 2 teaspoons baking powder
- 1/2 teaspoon baking soda
- 1/2 teaspoon salt
- 1 teaspoon poppyseeds
- 2 large eggs, slightly beaten
- 2/3 cup granulated sugar
- 1 teaspoon grated lemon zest
- 1/2 cup vegetable oil
- 1/2 cup low-fat buttermilk
- 2 tablespoons freshly-squeezed lemon juice

Instructions:

1. Preheat oven to 350 F. Grease an 8x8 inch or 11x7 inch baking pan with cooking spray.
2. In a medium bowl, whisk together flour, baking powder, baking soda, salt and poppyseed.
3. In a separate bowl, whisk together eggs, sugar, lemon zest, oil, buttermilk and lemon juice.
4. Add dry ingredients to wet ingredients and mix just until combined.
5. Pour batter into the prepared pan and bake for 40-45 minutes, or until a toothpick inserted into the center comes out clean.
6. Let cool in pan for 10 minutes before serving.

Nutrition Information:
Per Serving: Calories 329, Total Fat 15 g (Saturated fat 2 g), Cholesterol 35 mg, Sodium 282 mg, Potassium 107 mg, Total Carbohydrate 42 g (Dietary Fiber 1 g, Sugars 18 g), Protein 4 g.

17. Spice Bread

Spice Bread is a hearty and flavourful bread that is perfect for snacking or for pairing with a soup or salad. Loaded with warming cinnamon and nutmeg and the sweetness of raisins and currants, this is a loaf that will tantalize the taste buds.

Serving: 8-10 slices | Preparation Time: 15 minutes | Ready Time: 1 hour

Ingredients:
-2 cups all-purpose flour
-1 teaspoon baking soda
-1 teaspoon salt
-1 teaspoon ground cinnamon
-1/2 teaspoon ground nutmeg
-1/4 cup light brown sugar
-1 cup currants
-1 cup raisins
-2 eggs
-1/2 cup vegetable oil
-1 cup buttermilk

Instructions:
1. Preheat oven to 375F.
2. In a large bowl, whisk together the flour, baking soda, salt, cinnamon, nutmeg, and sugar.
3. Stir in the currants and raisins.
4. In a separate bowl, whisk together the eggs, oil, and buttermilk. Slowly pour the wet ingredients into the dry ingredients and stir until just combined.
5. Pour the batter into a greased 9-inch loaf pan.
6. Bake for 45-50 minutes, or until a toothpick inserted comes out clean.
7. Allow the bread to cool for 10 minutes before removing from the pan.

Nutrition Information (per slice):
Calories: 274 kcal, Fat: 11.2 g, Carbohydrates: 36.4 g, Protein: 4.3 g

18. Orange Almond Quick Bread

Crisp on the outside and light and fluffy on the inside, this orange almond quick bread is a bakery-worthy treat. It's a wonderful breakfast item or light dessert, with a subtle but delicious flavor combination of orange and almond that will have your family asking for more.

Serving: 8-10 slices | Preparation Time: 10 minutes | Ready Time: 50 minutes

Ingredients:
- 2 cups all-purpose flour
- 3/4 cup granulated sugar
- 2 teaspoons baking powder
- 1/2 teaspoon baking soda
- 1/4 teaspoon salt
- 1 large egg
- 1/2 cup vegetable oil
- 2/3 cup orange juice
- 2 tablespoons orange zest
- 3/4 cup sliced almonds

Instructions:
1. Preheat oven to 350 degrees F (175 degrees C). Grease an 8x4 inch loaf pan.
2. In a large bowl, combine flour, sugar, baking powder, baking soda, and salt.
3. In a separate large bowl, whisk together egg, oil, orange juice and zest.
4. Pour wet ingredients into dry ingredients and mix until just combined. Stir in almonds.
5. Pour batter into the prepared pan and spread evenly.
6. Bake for 45 to 50 minutes or until a toothpick inserted into the center comes out clean.

Nutrition Information: (per slice)
Calories: 223, Fat: 11.1g, Carbohydrates: 27.3g, Fiber: 1.1g, Protein: 3.9g

19. Toasted Coconut Bread

This Toasted Coconut Bread is a delicious, tropical-flavored tropical quick bread that is perfect for breakfast or a snack. It's moist, sweet and loaded with sweet shreds of coconut. Serve with some butter and a cup of your favorite coffee or tea for a special treat.

Serving: 12 | Preparation Time: 10 minutes | Ready Time: 50 minutes

Ingredients:
- 2 cups all-purpose flour
- 1 cup sugar
- 2 tsp baking powder
- 1 tsp salt
- 2 large eggs
- 1/3 cup unsalted butter, melted
- 1 cup coconut milk
- 1 cup sweetened shredded coconut

Instructions:
1. Preheat oven to 350 degrees. Grease a 9x5 inch loaf pan and set aside.
2. In a medium bowl, whisk together the flour, sugar, baking powder and salt.

3. In a separate bowl, whisk together the eggs, butter, and coconut milk.
4. Add the wet ingredients to the dry and mix until just combined. Fold in the shredded coconut.
5. Pour the batter into the prepared loaf pan and bake for 45 to 50 minutes, or until a toothpick inserted into the center comes out clean.
6. Allow the loaf to cool completely before serving.

Nutrition Information (Per Serving):
Calories: 271; Total Fat: 12.6 g; Cholesterol: 42 mg; Sodium: 133 mg; Total Carbohydrate: 34.8 g; Dietary Fiber: 1.7 g; Sugars: 16.9 g; Protein: 4.3 g.

20. Zucchini Carrot Bread

This moist and delicious Zucchini Carrot Bread is simple to make and full of amazing flavor! Its combination of zucchini and carrots make for a delectable and hearty texture, and its dense texture requires incredibly little baking time.

Serving: 8-10 | Preparation Time: 15 minutes | Ready Time: 1 hour

Ingredients:
   –   3 large carrots, grated
   –   2 eggs
   –   1 cup white sugar

Instructions:
1. Preheat oven to 350F (175°C). Grease a 9 x 5 inch loaf pan.
2. In a large bowl, beat eggs until smooth. Mix in sugar and then stir in the carrots and zucchini.
3. In a separate bowl, whisk together the flour, baking soda, salt and cinnamon. Slowly add the dry ingredients to the egg mixture and stir until just combined.
4. Pour the batter into the prepared pan. Bake in preheated oven for 55 minutes, or until a knife inserted into the center comes out clean.

Nutrition Information:

Per 1 slice (1/10 of loaf): Calories 207 kj, Protein 4g, Fat 1g, Carbohydrates 42g, Fibre 2g.

21. Maple Walnut Quick Bread

Maple Walnut Quick Bread is a delicious and easy-to-make sweet bread that perfect for a special breakfast treat or snack. This quick-bread tastes like sweet maple and toasted walnuts and will have your family asking for more.

Serving: 10 | Preparation Time: 15 minutes | Ready Time: 15 minutes

Ingredients:
- 2 cups all-purpose flour
- 2 teaspoon baking powder
- 1/2 teaspoon salt
- 1/2 cup butter (1 stick)
- 1/2 cups sugar
- 2 eggs
- 1/2 cup maple syrup
- 1/2 cup walnuts, chopped

Instructions:
1. Preheat the oven to 350 degrees F. Grease and flour a 9x5 inch loaf pan.
2. In a medium bowl, sift together the flour, baking powder, and salt.
3. In a large bowl, cream together the butter and sugar. Beat in the eggs, one at a time. Gradually add in the maple syrup and mix until combined.
4. Slowly fold the dry ingredients into the wet mix. Stir in the walnuts.
5. Pour the batter into the greased and floured loaf pan.
6. Bake for 40-45 minutes, or until a toothpick inserted in the center of the bread comes out clean.
7. Let cool before serving.

Nutrition Information (per slice):
Calories: 203, Fat: 8g, Protein: 3g, Carbohydrates: 29g, Sodium: 143 mg

22. Peach Bread

Peach Bread is a fruit-filled and subtly sweet quick bread that is easy to make and great as an afternoon snack.

Serving: 4-8 servings | Preparation Time: 15 mins | Ready Time: 15 min

Ingredients:
- 2 cups all-purpose flour
- 1 teaspoon baking soda
- 1/2 teaspoon salt
- 1/2 teaspoon ground cinnamon
- 1/2 cup vegetable oil
- 1 cup white sugar
- 2 eggs
- 1 teaspoon vanilla extract
- 2 cups mashed ripe peaches

Instructions:
1. Preheat oven to 350 degrees Fahrenheit. Grease an 8x4 inch loaf pan.
2. In a medium bowl, mix together flour, baking soda, salt and cinnamon.
3. In a separate large bowl, mix together oil, sugar, eggs, and vanilla extract.
4. Slowly stir in the flour mixture until just combined.
5. Fold in the mashed peaches until evenly distributed.
6. Pour batter into prepared pan.
7. Bake for 1 hour and 15 minutes, or until a toothpick inserted into the center comes out clean.
8. Allow to cool for 10-15 minutes before removing from pan to cool completely.

Nutrition Information:
Servings: 8-10, Calories: 245, Total Fat: 9.5g, Saturated Fat: 1.5 g, Protein: 3.5g, Total Carbs: 37.5g, Dietary Fiber: 1.2g, Sodium: 179mg

23. Chocolate Chip Bread

This delicious Chocolate Chip Bread is a tender, sweet yeasted bread studded with chocolate chips. With a simple list of ingredients, minimal | Preparation Time and only about an hour of rising time, this bread can be a delicious addition to any meal.

Serving: 12-15 servings | Preparation Time: 15 mins | Ready Time: 2 hrs

Ingredients:
- 3/4 cup lukewarm milk
- 2 and 1/4 teaspoons (1 package) active dry yeast
- 3/4 cup granulated sugar
- 2 teaspoons vanilla extract
- 6 tablespoons butter or margarine melted
- 3 eggs
- 4 and 1/4 cups all-purpose flour
- 1 teaspoon salt
- 2/3 cup semi-sweet chocolate chips

Instructions:
1. In a large bowl, combine the milk, yeast, sugar, and vanilla extract. Let stand for 5 minutes.
2. Add the melted butter, eggs, flour, and salt. Using an electric mixer, mix until fully combined. Dough will be wet, but if it's too sticky add up to 1/4 cup more flour.
3. Cover and let rise in a warm place for 1 hour.
4. Grease a 9x5-inch loaf pan. Punch down the dough, and knead in the chocolate chips.
5. Place the dough in the prepared pan, cover and let rise for 30 minutes.
6. Preheat the oven to 350F (175°C) and bake for 45-50 minutes, or until golden brown.
7. Remove from oven and let cool for 10-15 minutes before slicing and serving.

Nutrition Information:
Calories: 255, Fat: 10 g, Carbohydrates: 36 g, Protein: 5 g, Fiber: 1 g, Sugars: 15 g

24. Pumpkin Spice Bread

This delicious pumpkin spice bread is a fall favorite that is sure to please. The moist, flavorful bread with the sweet and savory combination of cinnamon, nutmeg and allspice is sure to tantalize your taste buds.

Serving: 1 loaf (16 slices) | Preparation Time: 15 minutes | Ready Time: 45 minutes

Ingredients:
- 2 1/2 cups all-purpose flour
- 1 teaspoon baking soda
- 1/4 teaspoon baking powder
- 1 teaspoon ground cinnamon
- 1/4 teaspoon ground ginger
- 1/4 teaspoon ground nutmeg
- 1/4 teaspoon allspice
- 1/4 teaspoon salt
- 1 cup unsalted butter, softened
- 1 1/2 cups brown sugar
- 4 eggs
- 2 teaspoons vanilla extract
- 1 15-ounce can solid-pack pumpkin puree

Instructions:
1. Preheat oven to 350F. Grease and flour a 9x5-inch loaf pan.
2. In a medium bowl, whisk together flour, baking soda, baking powder, cinnamon, ginger, nutmeg, allspice, and salt; set aside.
3. In a large bowl, cream together butter and brown sugar until light and fluffy. Add eggs one at a time, beating well after each addition. Beat in vanilla extract and pumpkin puree. Gradually add dry ingredients and mix until just combined.
4. Pour batter into prepared pan and bake for 40-45 minutes or until a toothpick inserted into the center comes out clean. Let cool for 10 minutes in the pan before turning out onto a wire cooling rack to cool completely.

Nutrition Information: per serving (1 slice):

Calories: 230 kcal, Fat: 11 g, Saturated fat: 7 g, Cholesterol: 57 mg, Sodium: 128 mg, Potassium: 114 mg, Carbohydrates: 27 g, Fiber: 1 g, Sugar: 13 g, Protein: 3.3 g.

25. Caramel Pecan Bread

Caramel Pecan Bread is a delicious twist on traditional bread. It is a filling, savory bread that is filled with chopped pecans, a creamy caramel sauce and a buttery tilt. Perfect for autumn or holiday celebrations, this savory bread is sure to be a hit with all your guests.

Serving: 10 slices | Preparation Time: 15 minutes | Ready Time: 55 minutes

Ingredients:
- 2 cups all-purpose flour
- 1 tablespoon baking powder
- 1 teaspoon salt
- 1/2 cup butter, softened
- 1/2 cup white sugar
- 2 eggs
- 1 cup evaporated milk
- 1/2 cup caramel sauce
- 1 cup chopped pecans

Instructions:
1. Preheat the oven to 350 degrees F (175 degrees C). Grease and flour a 9x5 inch loaf pan.
2. In a medium bowl, whisk together the flour, baking powder, and salt.
3. In a large bowl, cream the butter and sugar until light and fluffy. Beat in the eggs one at a time. Beat in the evaporated milk.
4. Gradually beat in the dry ingredients until thoroughly incorporated.
5. Pour half of the batter into the prepared pan. Drizzle with the caramel sauce and top with the chopped pecans. Pour the remaining batter over the top.
6. Bake for 45 minutes in the preheated oven, or until a toothpick inserted in the center comes out clean. Allow to cool before slicing.

Nutrition Information:
Calories: 312, Fat: 15Gr, Carbohydrates: 40g, Protein: 7g, Cholesterol: 57mg, Sodium: 199 mg, Potassium: 210 mg.

26. Banana Walnut Bread

Banana Walnut Bread is a sweet and nutty combination that makes a delicious and easy to make treat. It's a moist and flavorful loaf that's perfect for breakfast, snack or dessert.

Serving: 10-12 slices | Preparation Time: 10 minutes | Ready Time: 1 hour

Ingredients:
- 2 cups all-purpose flour
- 1 teaspoon baking soda
- 1/2 teaspoon salt
- 1/2 cup butter, softened
- 1 cup white sugar
- 2 eggs
- 1 teaspoon vanilla extract
- 2 cups mashed overripe bananas
- 1/2 cup chopped walnuts

Instructions:
1. Preheat oven to 350 degrees F (175 degrees C). Grease and flour a 9x5 inch loaf pan.
2. In a large bowl, combine flour, baking soda and salt.
3. In a separate bowl, cream together butter and sugar until light and fluffy. Beat in eggs one at a time, then stir in vanilla. Beat in the banana until mixture is creamy.
4. Add wet mixture to flour mixture and stir just until moistened. Stir in walnuts.
5. Pour batter into prepared loaf pan.
6. Bake in preheated oven for 60 minutes, until a toothpick inserted into center of the loaf comes out clean.

Nutrition Information:

Clockwise from left, Each serving contains 261 calories, 1.7 grams protein, 14.8 grams fat, 29.6 grams carbohydrates, 1.9 grams fiber, and 44.2 milligrams of cholesterol.

27. Almond Bread

Almond Bread is a delicious and healthy vegan bread prepared with almond meal, flaxseed meal and a variety of other wholesome ingredients. It is easy to make and bakes up quickly, making it an ideal bread to have on hand for sandwiches, toasts and snacks.

Serving: 12 slices | Preparation Time: 10 minutes | Ready Time: 35 minutes

Ingredients:
- 2 cups almond meal
- 1/4 cup ground flaxseed meal
- 2 tablespoons oil
- 1/4 teaspoon salt
- 2 tablespoons agave nectar
- 1 tablespoon baking powder
- 1 cup warm water

Instructions:
1. Preheat the oven to 350F.
2. Combine the almond meal, flaxseed meal, oil, salt, agave nectar and baking powder in a bowl.
3. Gradually stir in the water until a thick dough forms.
4. Grease a 9-inch loaf pan and turn the dough into the pan.
5. Bake for 30 to 35 minutes until the top is golden brown and a toothpick inserted into the center of the bread comes out clean.
6. Remove from the oven and let cool for 10 minutes before serving.

Nutrition Information:
Each slice of Almond Bread contains approximately 100 calories, 7.8 grams of fat, 5.4 grams of carbohydrates, and 3 grams of protein.

28. Coffee Cake

This delicious coffee cake will have your kitchen smelling amazing! With a rich and crumbly topping, this simple and easy cake is sure to tantalize your taste buds.

Serving: 10 slices | Preparation Time: 10 minutes | Ready Time: 1 hour

Ingredients:
- 2 cups all-purpose flour
- 1 cup sugar
- 2 teaspoons baking powder
- 1 teaspoon salt
- 1/4 cup butter, chilled and cut into small pieces
- 1 teaspoon ground cinnamon
- 1 teaspoon vanilla extract
- 1/2 cup buttermilk
- 2 eggs

Instructions:
1. Preheat the oven to 350 degrees F. Grease a 9-inch round cake pan.
2. In a large bowl, sift the flour, sugar, baking powder, and salt together. Cut in the butter until the mixture is crumbly.
3. Stir in the cinnamon, vanilla extract, buttermilk, and eggs until just blended.
4. Spread the batter into the prepared cake pan. Bake for 35 minutes or until golden brown.
5. Cool completely before serving.

Nutrition Information:
Serving Size: 1 slice, Calories: 200, Fat: 5g, Cholesterol: 40mg, Sodium: 350mg, Carbohydrates: 34g, Protein: 3g

29. Chocolate Swirl Bread

Chocolate Swirl Bread – Filling and delicious, this Chocolate Swirl Bread combines sweet chocolate and delicately spiced bread for a unique flavor that everyone is sure to enjoy.

Serving: 8 slices | Preparation Time: 15 minutes | Ready Time: 1 hour 10 minutes

Ingredients:

- 2 1/2 cups all-purpose flour
- 1 tablespoon baking powder
- 1/4 teaspoon baking soda
- 1/2 teaspoon ground cinnamon
- 1/4 teaspoon ground nutmeg
- 1/2 teaspoon sea salt
- 1/4 cup coconut oil, melted
- 5 tablespoons sucanat or other unrefined sugar
- 1 cup plain soymilk
- 2 teaspoons pure vanilla extract
- 1/4 cup raw cacao powder
- 2 tablespoons pure maple syrup

Instructions:

1. Preheat the oven to 375F. Grease the bottom and sides of an 8x4-inch loaf pan with coconut oil.
2. In a large bowl, mix together the flour, baking powder, baking soda, cinnamon, nutmeg, and sea salt until blended.
3. Add the coconut oil, sucanat/sugar, soymilk, and vanilla extract. Stir until blended.
4. In a medium bowl, mix together the cacao powder and maple syrup.
5. Pour half the batter into the prepared loaf pan. Add the chocolate mixture and spread it out evenly. Add remaining the batter, making sure to cover the chocolate mixture.
6. Bake in preheated oven for 50-60 minutes. Test with a toothpick to make sure it comes out clean before removing it from the oven.

Nutrition Information:

Serving size: 1 slice (1/8 of loaf), Calories: 220 kcal, Carbohydrates: 36g, Protein: 3.5g, Fat: 8g, Sugar: 7g, Fiber: 2g, Cholesterol 0 mg, Sodium: 245mg

30. Honey Wheat Bread

Honey Wheat Bread is a sweet and tasty variation on classic wheat bread. It is made with honey, whole wheat flour, and other simple ingredients. It is easy to make and makes for a great sandwich bread.

Serving: Makes 1 loaf, 10-12 slices | Preparation Time: 15 minutes | Ready Time: 1 hour

Ingredients:
- 1.5 cups of whole wheat flour
- 1 teaspoon of baking powder
- 1 teaspoon of salt
- 1 tablespoon of vegetable oil
- 1/2 cup of honey
- 1/2 cup of warm water
- 1 teaspoon of active dry yeast

Instructions:
1. Preheat the oven to 375 degrees.
2. In a bowl combine the whole wheat flour, baking powder, salt, oil and honey.
3. In a separate bowl, dissolve the active dry yeast in the warm water and let stand for 5 minutes.
4. Add the yeast mixture to the flour mixture and stir until combined.
5. Transfer the dough to a greased loaf pan and let rise for about 30 minutes.
6. Bake for about 30 minutes or until the top is golden brown.
7. Let the bread cool for 10-15 minutes before slicing.

Nutrition Information:
Serving size: 1 slice, 193 calories, 4g fat, 38g carbohydrates, 4g protein.

31. Molasses Gingerbread

Molasses Gingerbread - This classic gingerbread cake is made with sweet spiced molasses, giving it a unique and delicious flavor. This cake is sure to become a family favorite!

Serving: 8 | Preparation Time: 15 minutes | Ready Time: 1 hour

Ingredients:
- 2 cups all-purpose flour
- 1 tablespoon baking soda
- 2 teaspoons ground ginger
- 1 teaspoon ground cinnamon
- 1/4 teaspoon ground cloves
- 3/4 cup butter
- 3/4 cup molasses
- 1/4 cup packed brown sugar
- 1/4 cup white sugar
- 1 egg
- 1/2 cup buttermilk

Instructions:
1. Preheat oven to 350 degrees F (175 degrees C). Grease and flour 8×8 inch baking pan.
2. In a medium bowl, sift together the flour, baking soda, ground ginger, cinnamon, and cloves.
3. In a large bowl, cream together the butter, molasses, brown sugar, and white sugar until smooth. Beat in the egg until combined, then stir in the buttermilk.
4. Gradually stir in the sifted ingredients, mixing until just combined.
5. Spread the batter into the prepared pan.
6. Bake for 30 minutes in the preheated oven, until a toothpick inserted into the center of the cake comes out clean.

Nutrition Information:
Per Serving (1/8 of recipe): Calories: 255, Fat: 10g, Cholesterol: 37mg, Sodium: 209mg, Carbohydrates: 38g, Protein: 3.2g

32. Cranberry Walnut Bread

This Cranberry Walnut Bread is a sweet, delicious treat that is perfect for any occasion. It is a moist and fluffy loaf of bread studded with tart cranberries and crunchy walnuts.

Serving: Makes one 9x5-inch loaf - 10 slices | Preparation Time: 15 minutes | Ready Time: 75 minutes

Ingredients:
-1 1/2 cups all-purpose flour
-1 cup white sugar
-1/2 teaspoon salt
-1 teaspoon baking powder
-1/3 cup vegetable oil
-1/3 cup orange juice
-2 eggs
-1 teaspoon vanilla extract
-1 cup fresh cranberries
-1/2 cup chopped walnuts

Instructions:
1. Preheat oven to 350 degrees F (175 degrees C). Grease a 9x5 inch loaf pan.
2. In a medium bowl, mix together the flour, sugar, salt and baking powder.
3. In a large bowl, mix together the oil, orange juice, eggs and vanilla.
4. Stir the dry ingredients into the wet ingredients. Fold in the cranberries and walnuts.
5. Pour batter into the prepared loaf pan.
6. Bake for about 60 to 75 minutes, until a knife inserted into the center comes out clean.

Nutrition Information:
Calories: 184, Protein: 3g, Carbohydrates: 25g, Fat: 8g

33. Chocolate Peanut Butter Swirl Bread

Chocolate Peanut Butter Swirl Bread is an irresistibly delicious combination of two of your favorite things. With delicious peanut butter and chocolate flavors combined into one, this bread is the perfect treat for special occasions.

Serving: 10 | Preparation Time: 30 minutes | Ready Time: 1 hour

Ingredients:
- 1 1/2 cups all-purpose flour
- 2 tsp. baking powder
- 1/4 tsp. salt
- 2 Tbs. cocoa powder
- 2 Tbs. sugar
- 1/4 cups creamy peanut butter
- 1/2 cups milk
- 2 eggs
- 2 Tbs. melted butter

Instructions:
1. Preheat the oven to 350F (180°C). Grease a 9x5-inch loaf pan and set aside.
2. In a large bowl, whisk together the flour, baking powder, salt, cocoa powder, and sugar.
3. In a separate bowl, mix together the peanut butter, milk, eggs, and melted butter until combined.
4. Pour the wet ingredients into the dry ingredients and stir until combined.
5. Pour half of the batter into the greased loaf pan.
6. Drop small spoonfuls of the remaining batter onto the top of the batter in the loaf pan.
7. Using a butter knife, swirl the spoonfuls of peanut butter in the batter.
8. Bake in the preheated oven for 40 to 45 minutes, or until a toothpick inserted into the center comes out clean.
9. Let the bread cool for 10 minutes before removing from the pan and cutting into slices.

Nutrition Information:
Calories: 347, Fat: 16.7g, Saturated Fat: 6.9g, Trans Fat: 0g, Cholesterol: 67mg, Sodium: 227mg, Carbohydrates: 41.2g, Fiber: 2.9g, Sugar: 10.4g, Protein: 9.4g.

34. Apple Walnut Bread

Apple Walnut Bread is a delicious and moist quick bread recipe that is full of sweet apples and decadent walnuts. An easy and delicious treat for breakfast or snack, this Apple Walnut Bread is sure to be a family favorite!

Serving: 10 | Preparation Time: 20 minutes | Ready Time: 1 hour

Ingredients:
-1 1/2 cups all-purpose flour
-1 1/2 teaspoons baking powder
-1/2 teaspoon baking soda
-1/4 teaspoon salt
-1/2 cup firmly packed light brown sugar
-2 large eggs
-3/4 cup buttermilk
-1/4 cup vegetable oil
-1 teaspoon vanilla extract
-1 cup diced peeled apples (2 to 3 medium apples)
-1/2 cup walnuts, coarsely chopped

Instructions:
1. Preheat oven to 350 degrees F. Grease an 8-by-4-inch loaf pan.
2. In a medium bowl, whisk together the flour, baking powder, baking soda, and salt.
3. In a large bowl, whisk together the brown sugar and eggs until combined. Whisk in the buttermilk, oil, and vanilla.
4. Pour the wet ingredients over the dry ingredients, and stir until just combined. Fold in the apples and walnuts.
5. Pour the batter into the prepared pan.
6. Bake until a cake tester inserted into the center of the loaf comes out clean, about 45 to 50 minutes.
7. Transfer the pan to a cooling rack and cool for 10 minutes before turning the loaf out onto the rack to cool completely.

Nutrition Information:

Serving Size: 1 slice, Calories: 180, Fat: 8g, Carbohydrates: 24g, Protein: 3g, Sodium: 80mg, Cholesterol: 30mg

35. Sweet Potato Bread

This Sweet Potato Bread is a comforting and healthy treat that combines the sweetness of sweet potatoes and the nuttiness of whole wheat flour to create a delicious loaf of bread.

Serving: 8-10 | Preparation Time: 15 minutes | Ready Time: 60 minutes.

Ingredients:
- 2 cups mashed sweet potato
- 1/4 cup softened butter
- 1/4 cup honey
- 2 eggs
- 2 cups whole wheat flour
- 1 teaspoon baking soda
- 1 teaspoon baking powder
- 1 teaspoon ground cinnamon

Instructions:
1. Preheat the oven to 350F.
2. In a large bowl, cream together the butter, honey and eggs until light and fluffy.
3. In a separate bowl, mix together the mashed sweet potatoes, whole wheat flour, baking soda, baking powder and ground cinnamon.
4. Slowly add the wet ingredients to the dry ingredients and mix until just combined.
5. Pour the batter into a greased loaf pan and bake for 50-60 minutes, or until a toothpick inserted into the center comes out clean.

Nutrition Information:
Nutritional facts per serving (1 slice):
Calories: 144; Total Fat: 3.6g; Saturated Fat: 1.8g; Sodium: 97mg; Total Carbohydrates: 25.1g; Dietary Fiber: 2.1g; Total Sugar: 10.6g; Protein: 3.2g

36. Cinnamon Swirl Bread

Cinnamon Swirl Bread is a deliciously spiced and sweet breakfast treat. This quick and easy recipe makes a perfect breakfast or a tasty snack.

Serving 8-10 pieces | Preparation Time: 10 minutes | Ready Time: 70 minutes

Ingredients:
- 1 cup packed brown sugar
- 2 tablespoons ground cinnamon
- 1/2 cup butter, softened
- 2 8-oz cans Pillsbury® refrigerated crescent dinner rolls
- 1/2 cup finely chopped walnuts (optional)

Instructions:
1. Preheat oven to 350F. Grease a 9-inch tart or round cake pan.
2. In a small bowl, mix together the brown sugar and cinnamon.
3. Spread the butter over the bottom and slightly up the sides of the prepared cake pan.
4. Sprinkle the sugar and cinnamon mixture evenly over the butter, reserving some for later.
5. Separate the crescent rolls and coat each triangle with the cinnamon-sugar mixture. Roll up each triangle and arrange them in the buttered cake pan. Sprinkle any remaining cinnamon-sugar mixture over the top.
6. Bake for 30 minutes or until golden brown.
7. Let cool for 5 minutes before slicing and serving.

Nutrition Information:
Each serving (1 piece) of Cinnamon Swirl Bread contains 247 calories, 13.6g of fat, and 28.6g of carbohydrates.

37. Caramel Apple Bread

This caramel apple bread is the perfect combination of sweet and tart – a delicious dessert that's ready in no time.

Serving: 6-8 | Preparation Time: 10 minutes | Ready Time: 60 minutes

Ingredients:
- 2 eggs
- 2 cups all-purpose flour
- 1 cup white sugar
- 1 teaspoon baking powder
- 1/2 teaspoon baking soda
- 1/2 teaspoon salt
- 2 1/2 cup apples, peeled and chopped
- 1 teaspoon ground cinnamon
- 1/2 cup melted butter
- 1/2 cup caramel sauce

Instructions:
1. Preheat oven to 350 degrees F. Grease a 9x5 inch loaf pan.
2. In a large bowl, beat together eggs, butter and sugar.
3. In a separate bowl, sift together flour, baking powder, baking soda and salt. Add the dry ingredients to the wet ingredients until just combined.
4. Stir in the apples and cinnamon.
5. Transfer batter to the prepared loaf pan and pour caramel sauce over top.
6. Bake for 55 to 60 minutes or until a toothpick inserted near the center of the loaf comes out clean.

Nutrition Information:
Calories: 213; Fat: 7g; Sodium: 199mg; Carbohydrates: 32g; Fiber: 1g; Protein: 3g

38. Maple Cinnamon Bread

This Maple Cinnamon Bread is the perfect way to start your day or make a special brunch. The maple glaze brings out the flavors of the sweet cinnamon bread, making it an irresistible treat!

Serving: 8 slices | Preparation Time: 10 minutes | Ready Time: 60 minutes

Ingredients:
- 2 1/2 cups all-purpose flour
- 1/4 cup butter, softened
- 1 cup packed brown sugar
- 1 teaspoon ground cinnamon
- 2/3 cup milk
- 1 teaspoon baking powder
- 1/2 teaspoon baking soda
- 1/4 teaspoon salt
- 1 egg
- 2 tablespoons real maple syrup
- Topping
- 1/4 cup buter, softened
- 2 tablespoons real maple syrup
- 1/4 cup packed brown sugar
- 2 teaspoons ground cinnamon

Instructions:
1. Preheat oven to 350F (175°C) and lightly grease a 9x5 inch loaf pan.
2. In a large mixing bowl, cream together the butter and brown sugar. Stir in the egg, milk, maple syrup, and mix until smooth.
3. Whisk together the flour, baking powder, baking soda, and salt in a separate bowl. Gently stir the dry ingredients into the wet until just combined.
4. Spread the batter into the greased pan. In a separate bowl, mix together the topping ingredients. Sprinkle over the top of the bread.
5. Bake for 50-60 minutes, or until a toothpick inserted into the center of the bread comes out clean. Let cool before slicing.

Nutrition Information:
Calories: 290kcal, Carbohydrates: 42g, Protein: 3g, Fat: 12g, Saturated Fat: 7g, Sodium: 259mg, Potassium: 105mg, Fiber: 1g, Sugar: 24g, Vitamin A: 416IU, Calcium: 50mg, Iron: 1mg.

39. Banana Chocolate Chip Bread

Intoducing Banana Chocolate Chip Bread, an irresistible sweet and savory treat! This delicious bread is perfect for breakfast or a snack, and perfect for any banana lover.

Serving: 10 slices | Preparation Time: 10 minutes | Ready Time: 55 minutes.

Ingredients:
-3 ripe bananas
-1/3 cup melted butter
-1 teaspoon baking soda
-Pinch of salt
-1 cup sugar
-1 egg, beaten
-1 teaspoon vanilla extract
-1 1/2 cups of all-purpose flour
-1/2 cup semi-sweet chocolate chips

Instructions:
1. Preheat the oven to 350F (175°C). Grease a 9 x 5 inch loaf pan with butter or cooking spray.
2. In a large bowl, mash the bananas, then mix in the melted butter.
3. Stir in the baking soda and salt, then mix in the sugar, egg, and vanilla.
4. Gently stir in the flour until it's just combined, then mix in the chocolate chips.
5. Pour the batter into the prepared loaf pan, and bake for 45-55 minutes, or until a toothpick inserted in the center comes out clean.
6. Let cool for 10 minutes before turning out onto a cooling rack.

Nutrition Information:
200 calories, 8g fat, 32g carbohydrates, 2g protein per slice.

40. Fig Nut Quick Bread

This Fig Nut Quick Bread is a delicious, moist and flavorful quick bread that comes together with only a few ingredients. Studded with flavorful figs and crunchy nuts, this quick bread can be enjoyed for breakfast, snack, or dessert.

Serving: 10-12 slices | Preparation Time: 15 minutes | Ready Time: 1 hour

Ingredients:
- 2 cups all-purpose flour
- 4 teaspoons baking powder
- 1 teaspoon salt
- 1/2 teaspoon ground cinnamon
- 1/4 cup vegetable oil
- 1 cup granulated sugar
- 2 eggs
- 1 teaspoon vanilla extract
- 1 cup milk
- 3/4 cup chopped dried figs
- 3/4 cup chopped nuts

Instructions:
1. Preheat oven to 350F degrees. Grease an 8×4-inch loaf pan.
2. In a medium bowl, whisk together flour, baking powder, salt and cinnamon.
3. In a large bowl, combine oil, sugar, eggs and vanilla. Beat until blended.
4. Add dry ingredients and milk alternately, starting and ending with the dry ingredients. Beat until blended.
5. Fold in figs and chopped nuts.
6. Pour batter into prepared loaf pan.
7. Bake for 45-55 minutes, or until a toothpick inserted into the center comes out clean.
8. Cool completely before slicing and serving.

Nutrition Information:
Per slice: 200 calories; 9 g fat; 27 g carbohydrates; 4 g protein; 1 g fiber; 10 mg cholesterol; 180 mg sodium.

41. Pumpkin Chocolate Chip Bread

Pumpkin Chocolate Chip Bread is an incredibly moist, buttery pumpkin bread enriched with chocolate chips, cinnamon and nutmeg. The perfect all-in-one bread solution with a delicious seasonal flavor, it's sure to become a new favorite!

Serving: 10-12 slices | Preparation Time: 15 minutes | Ready Time: 1 hour

Ingredients:
- 2 cups all-purpose flour
- 1 teaspoon baking powder
- 1/2 teaspoon baking soda
- 1/2 teaspoon salt
- 1 teaspoon ground cinnamon
- 1/2 teaspoon ground nutmeg
- 2/3 cup vegetable oil
- 1 cup light or dark brown sugar
- 2 large eggs
- 1 cup canned pumpkin puree
- 1/2 cup mini semi-sweet chocolate chips

Instructions:
1. Preheat the oven to 350F. Grease a 9×5-inch loaf pan with nonstick cooking spray.
2. In a medium bowl, whisk together the flour, baking powder, baking soda, salt, cinnamon and nutmeg.
3. In a large bowl, blend the oil, brown sugar and eggs until creamy.
4. Add in the pumpkin puree and stir until incorporated.
5. Gradually add in the flour mixture, stirring until everything is combined.
6. Fold in the chocolate chips.
7. Transfer the batter to the prepared loaf pan and smooth the top.
8. Bake for 50-60 minutes, until a toothpick inserted into the center of the loaf comes out clean.
9. Let the bread cool in the pan for 10 minutes before transferring to a wire rack to cool completely.

Nutrition Information:
Calories: 242; Fat: 11g; Sodium: 162mg; Carbohydrates: 31g; Fiber: 2g; Protein: 3g

42. Strawberry Bread

This Strawberry Bread is a sweet, fragrant quick bread made with fresh strawberries, flour, and sugar. Perfect for a snack or a special breakfast treat, this delicious bread is sure to delight!

Serving: 8-10 slices | Preparation Time: 10 minutes | Ready Time: 1 hour

Ingredients:
- 2 cups all-purpose flour
- 2 tsp baking powder
- 1/2 tsp baking soda
- 1/2 tsp salt
- 1 cup white sugar
- 1/2 cup butter, softened
- 2 eggs
- 3/4 cup milk
- 1 cup chopped fresh strawberries

Instructions:
1. Preheat oven to 350 degrees F. Grease a 9x5 inch loaf pan.
2. In a large bowl, mix together flour, baking powder, baking soda, salt, and sugar.
3. In a small bowl, cream together the butter and eggs.
4. Add the wet ingredients to the dry ingredients and mix until smooth.
5. Fold in the chopped strawberries.
6. Pour batter into prepared pan and bake for 45-50 minutes, or until a toothpick inserted into the center of the loaf comes out clean.
7. Let cool for 10 minutes before removing from pan. Slice and enjoy!

Nutrition Information (per serving):
Calories: 198, Total Fat: 8.4 g, Saturated Fat: 4.9 g, Cholesterol: 39 mg, Sodium: 202 mg, Total Carbohydrates: 27.6 g, Dietary Fiber: 1.2 g, Sugars: 14.1 g, Protein: 3.2 g.

43. Red Velvet Bread

Red Velvet Bread is a simple bread recipe with a rich red color. It's a perfectly sweet cakey bread that makes a tasty breakfast treat or a festive addition to any table.

Serving: 8-10 | Preparation Time: 20 minutes | Ready Time: 1 hour

Ingredients:
- 2 1/2 cups all-purpose flour
- 1/3 cup granulated sugar
- 2 teaspoons baking powder
- 2 tablespoons cocoa powder
- 1/2 teaspoon baking soda
- 1 teaspoon salt
- 1/2 cup butter, melted and cooled
- 1 cup buttermilk
- 1 teaspoon pure vanilla extract
- 1 1/2 teaspoons white vinegar
- 2 large eggs
- 2 Tablespoons red food coloring

Instructions:
1. Preheat oven to 350 degrees F. Grease and flour a 8-x5-inch loaf pan.
2. In a medium bowl, add in all-purpose flour, sugar, baking powder, cocoa powder, baking soda, and salt then whisk together.
3. In a separate bowl, whisk together melted butter, buttermilk, vanilla extract, vinegar, eggs, and red food coloring until well combined.
4. Add wet ingredients to dry ingredients, and stir until just combined. Do not overmix.
5. Pour batter into loaf pan, and bake for 35 to 40 minutes, or until a toothpick inserted into the center of the loaf comes out clean.
6. Allow the bread to cool in the pan for 10 minutes, before removing it to cool completely.

Nutrition Information:
Per serving (1 slice): 253 calories; 11.9 g fat; 28.6 g carbohydrates; 4.2 g protein

44. Lemon Raspberry Bread

This delicious Lemon Raspberry Bread combines sweet raspberries and tart lemons for a flavor-packed, zesty delight! There's no better way to start off your day than with a slice (or two!) of this unique breakfast bread.

Serving: 10-12 slices | Preparation Time: 10 minute | Ready Time: 60 minutes.

Ingredients:
-2 3/4 cups all-purpose flour
-1/2 cup granulated sugar
-1 teaspoon salt
-2 teaspoons baking powder
-1 cup buttermilk
-1/4 cup + 2 tablespoons vegetable oil
-2 eggs
-Zest of 2 lemons
-Juice of 1 lemon
-1 cup fresh raspberries
-Turbinado sugar, for garnish

Instructions:
1. Preheat the oven to 350F. Grease a 9"x5" loaf pan and set aside.
2. In a medium mixing bowl, whisk together the flour, sugar, salt, baking powder, and lemon zest.
3. In a separate bowl, mix together the buttermilk, vegetable oil, eggs, and lemon juice.
4. Pour the wet ingredients into the dry and mix until just combined. Add in the raspberries, and gently stir them in.
5. Pour the batter into the prepared loaf pan, and sprinkle the top with turbinado sugar.
6. Bake for 55-65 minutes, until a toothpick inserted into the center of the bread comes out clean. Allow to cool before slicing and serving.

Nutrition Information (roughly per slice):
Calories: 171; Fat: 7g; Saturated Fat: 3g; Cholesterol: 29mg; Sodium: 192mg; Carbohydrates: 25g; Fiber: 1g; Sugar: 8g; Protein: 3g

45. Zucchini Chocolate Chip Bread

This delicious and simple Zucchini Chocolate Chip Bread is a great way to increase the nutrient content of your bread while still enjoying the sweetness of chocolate chips.

Serving: 8 slices | Preparation Time: 15 minutes | Ready Time: 1 hour

Ingredients:
-1 cup all-purpose flour
-3/4 teaspoon baking soda
-1/4 teaspoon baking powder
-1/4 teaspoon salt
-1 teaspoon ground cinnamon
-3/4 cup brown sugar
-1/4 cup butter, melted
-1/4 cup applesauce
-2 eggs
-1 teaspoon vanilla extract
-1 cup zucchini, shredded
-1/2 cup semi-sweet chocolate chips

Instructions:
1. Preheat oven to 350 degrees F. Grease an 8x4 inch loaf pan.
2. In a medium sized bowl, whisk together flour, baking soda, baking powder, salt, and cinnamon.
3. In a large bowl, beat together brown sugar, butter, applesauce, eggs, and vanilla extract until smooth.
4. Add the dry ingredients to the wet ingredients, and mix until just incorporated.
5. Gently stir in the zucchini and chocolate chips.
6. Pour batter into the prepared pan, smoothing out the top.
7. Bake for 40-50 minutes, or until a toothpick inserted in the center comes out clean.
8. Let cool in the pan for 10 minutes before transferring to a wire rack to cool completely.

Nutrition Information:

Per slice: 230 calories, 10 g fat (5 g saturated fat), 46 mg sodium, 32 g carbohydrate, 1 g fiber, 21 g sugar, 3 g protein.

46. Carrot Pineapple Bread

This Carrot Pineapple Bread recipe is a perfect balance of sweet and savory. It's moist, fluffy, and perfectly spiced. Made with carrots, pineapple, sugar, banana, and a few other simple ingredients, this is a tasty, comforting treat that's sure to be a hit!

Serving: 8 | Preparation Time: 10 minutes

Ingredients:
-2 cups all-purpose flour
-2 teaspoon baking powder
-1 teaspoon baking soda
-1/2 teaspoon salt
-1 teaspoon ground cinnamon
-1/4 teaspoon ground nutmeg
-3/4 cup sugar
-1/3 cup vegetable oil
-2 eggs
-1/2 cup mashed banana
-1/2 cup grated carrots
-1/2 cup crushed pineapple
-1/2 cup chopped walnuts

Instructions:
1. Preheat oven to 350 degrees. Grease and flour a 9x5 inch loaf pan.
2. In a large bowl, mix together flour, baking powder, baking soda, salt, cinnamon, nutmeg, and sugar.
3. In a separate bowl, mix together oil, eggs, banana, carrots, pineapple, and walnuts.
4. Add wet ingredients to dry ingredients and stir until just combined. Do not overmix.
5. Pour batter into prepared pan and bake for about 55 minutes, or until a toothpick inserted into the center of the bread comes out clean.

6. Cool in the pan for 10 minutes, then turn out onto a wire rack to cool completely.

Nutrition Information:
Calories: 272, Total Fat: 11.5g, Saturated Fat: 2.6g, Cholesterol: 37mg, Sodium: 174mg, Total Carbohydrate: 36.2g, Dietary Fiber: 1.6g, Sugars: 19.6g, Protein: 3.7g

47. Banana Oat Bread

Banana oat bread is a delicious and healthy bread recipe made with whole grain oats and ripe bananas. A perfect snack or breakfast, this moist and tasty quick bread comes together in a snap! Serve it with butter and honey, or as is for a healthy snack.

Serving: 1 loaf | Preparation Time: 15 minutes | Ready Time: 50 minutes

Ingredients:
- 1 1/2 cups old fashioned oats
- 2 cups self-rising flour
- 1 teaspoon baking soda
- 1 teaspoon ground cinnamon
- Pinch of salt
- 3 ripe bananas, mashed
- 1/2 cup sour cream or plain yogurt
- 1 cup white sugar
- 1 teaspoon vanilla extract
- 2 large eggs

Instructions:
1. Preheat oven to 350F. Grease a 9-inch loaf pan and set aside.
2. In a medium bowl, mix together oats, flour, baking soda, cinnamon, and salt.
3. In a separate bowl, mix together bananas, sour cream, sugar, vanilla, and eggs.

4. Slowly add the dry ingredients to the wet ingredients, stirring until just combined.
5. Transfer batter to the loaf pan and bake for 45-50 minutes, or until a toothpick inserted into the center comes out clean.
6. Let cool on a wire rack for 15 minutes before serving.

Nutrition Information:
400 calories, 8g fat, 76g carbohydrates, 4.5g protein

48. Cranberry Orange Walnut Bread

This moist and flavorful Cranberry Orange Walnut Bread is the perfect holiday treat, combining sweet and tart flavors with crunchy walnuts. Serve as breakfast, snack, or dessert; thisbread is sure to become a family favorite.

Serving: 10 slices | Preparation Time: 15 minutes | Ready Time: 1 hour 15 minutes

Ingredients:
- 2 cups all-purpose flour
- 1 cup white sugar
- 3/4 teaspoon baking soda
- 1/2 teaspoon salt
- 1/2 teaspoon ground nutmeg
- 1/4 cup butter
- 2 eggs, lightly beaten
- 2 tablespoons orange zest
- Juice of 1 orange
- 1/2 cup buttermilk
- 1 1/2 cups fresh or frozen cranberries
- 1/2 cup chopped walnuts

Instructions:
1. Preheat oven to 350°. Grease a 9x5 inch loaf pan; set aside.
2. In a large bowl, whisk together flour, sugar, baking soda, salt and nutmeg. Cut in butter until mixture resembles coarse crumbs.

3. In a second bowl, combine eggs, orange zest, orange juice and buttermilk. Add to flour mixture and stir just until blended. Gently fold in cranberries and walnuts.

4. Pour mixture into prepared pan and bake for 1 hour and 15 minutes, or until a toothpick inserted in the center comes out clean. Cool in pan for 10 minutes before turning out onto a wire rack to cool completely.

Nutrition Information:
Calories: 230; Total fat: 9g; Saturated fat: 4g; Cholesterol: 50mg; Sodium: 200mg; Carbohydrates: 32g; Protein: 4g; Fiber: 2g.

49. Chocolate Orange Bread

This sweet and decadent Chocolate Orange Bread is an easy and delicious treat that can be served for breakfast, dessert, or any time in between. Serve it warm with a bit of butter and gooey orange flavoured ganache for an extra special indulgence.

Serving: 8-12 | Preparation Time: 10 minutes | Ready Time: 1 hour 10 minutes

Ingredients:
- 2 cups all-purpose flour
- 2 teaspoons baking powder
- 1/4 teaspoon salt
- 1/2 cup (1 stick) unsalted butter, melted and cooled
- 1/4 cup granulated sugar
- 1/4 cup dark cocoa powder
- 2 eggs
- 1 teaspoon vanilla extract
- 1/4 cup orange marmalade
- 1/4 cup dark chocolate chips

Instructions:
1. Preheat oven to 350F (175C). Grease a 9 x 5-inch loaf pan and line with parchment paper.
2. In a large bowl, whisk together the flour, baking powder and salt.

3. In a separate bowl, whisk together the melted butter and sugar. Whisk in the cocoa powder until combined.
4. Add the eggs, one at a time, whisking until combined. Whisk in the vanilla extract.
5. Add the wet mixture to the dry ingredients and stir until just combined.
6. Spread the batter into the prepared pan and spread the marmalade and dark chocolate chips over the top.
7. Bake for 55-60 minutes, or until a toothpick inserted into the center comes out clean. Let cool in the pan for 10 minutes before transferring to a cooling rack.

Nutrition Information:
Serving Size: 1 slice, Calories: 348, Fat: 16g, Carbohydrates: 45g, Protein: 5g, Sodium: 162mg, Cholesterol: 51mg

50. Pear Bread

Pear Bread is a delicious, sweet, quick bread that makes a perfect addition to any meal. This easy-to-make bread is filled with flavorful pears and spices that will make your house smell amazing. Serve it warm with butter or cream cheese for breakfast or as a dessert.

Serving: 12 slices | Preparation Time: 15 minutes | Ready Time: 1 hour 20 minutes

Ingredients:
- 2 cups all-purpose flour
- 2 teaspoons baking powder
- 1/4 teaspoon salt
- 1/2 cup packed brown sugar
- 1 teaspoon ground cinnamon
- 1/4 teaspoon ground nutmeg
- 1/2 cup vegetable oil
- 2 large eggs
- 2 teaspoons almond extract
- 2 cups peeled and diced pear

Instructions:
1. Preheat oven to 350F. Grease and flour a 9x5" loaf pan.
2. In a medium bowl, whisk together the flour, baking powder and salt.
3. In a large bowl, whisk together the brown sugar, cinnamon and nutmeg.
4. Add in the vegetable oil, eggs and almond extract and whisk until well combined.
5. Add the dry ingredients to the wet ingredients and stir until just combined.
6. Fold in the diced pear pieces.
7. Spread batter into prepared pan and bake for 1 hour 20 minutes or until a toothpick inserted into the center comes out with a few crumbs.
8. Allow to cool for at least 15 minutes before slicing and serving.

Nutrition Information:
Calories: 258 kcal, Carbohydrates: 33 g, Protein: 3 g, Fat:13 g, Saturated Fat: 10 g, Cholesterol: 31 mg, Sodium: 145 mg, Potassium: 128 mg, Fiber: 1 g, Sugar: 16 g, Vitamin A: 55 IU, Vitamin C: 1 mg, Calcium: 48 mg, Iron: 1.5 mg

51. Lemon Blueberry Bread

This delicious Lemon Blueberry Bread is an amazing combination of subtly sweet and tart flavors. It makes a wonderful breakfast, snack, or dessert. It can easily be made into muffins as well.

Serving: 8-10 slices | Preparation Time: 10 minutes | Ready Time: 60 minutes

Ingredients:
- 2 cups all-purpose flour
- 1 teaspoon baking powder
- 1 teaspoon baking soda
- 1/2 teaspoon salt
- 3/4 cup granulated sugar
- Zest of 1 lemon
- 1/2 cup vegetable oil

- 2 large eggs
- 1/2 cup whole milk
- 1 teaspoon pure vanilla extract
- 1–2 cups fresh or frozen blueberries

Instructions:
1. Preheat oven to 350F and prepare a 9×5-inch loaf pan by greasing it or lining it with parchment paper.
2. In a medium bowl, whisk together flour, baking powder, baking soda, and salt.
3. In a separate large bowl, whisk together sugar, lemon zest, oil, eggs, milk, and vanilla until combined.
4. Slowly add dry ingredients to the wet ingredients and stir until just combined. Do not overmix.
5. Gently fold in blueberries.
6. Transfer batter to prepared loaf pan and bake for 50–60 minutes, or until a toothpick inserted into the center comes out clean.
7. Allow to cool in the pan for 10 minutes, then transfer to a wire rack to cool completely.

Nutrition Information: (Per Serving)
Calories – 295, Fat - 10g, Carbohydrates - 45g, Protein - 4g, Sodium - 280mg, Fiber - 1g

52. Lemon Poppyseed Pound Cake

This zesty Lemon Poppyseed Pound Cake is an easy and delicious recipe that will have your family and friends begging for more. It has a moist and fluffy crumb flecked with subtle bursts of tart citrus, and the addition of poppyseeds adds a crunchy and nutty complexity.

Servings: 8 | Preparation Time: 10 minutes | Ready Time: 1 hour

Ingredients:
- 1/2 cup unsalted butter, room temperature
- 1 cup granulated sugar
- 2 large eggs
- 1 Tablespoon fresh lemon zest

- 1 teaspoon fresh lemon juice
- 1 teaspoon vanilla extract
- 1 3/4 cups all-purpose flour
- 2 teaspoons baking powder
- 1/4 teaspoon salt
- 1/2 cup milk
- 2 Tablespoons poppyseeds
- Powdered sugar, for dusting

Instructions:
1. Preheat oven to 350F and grease a 9×5 inch loaf pan.
2. Beat butter and sugar together in a large bowl until light and fluffy, about 3 minutes.
3. Add eggs, lemon zest, lemon juice and vanilla extract, mix until blended.
4. In a separate bowl, mix together flour, baking powder, and salt.
5. Slowly add half of the dry ingredients to the wet ingredients, mix until just combined, then add milk and remaining dry ingredients.
6. Fold in poppyseeds and pour into prepared pan.
7. Bake in preheated oven for 45-50 minutes, or until a toothpick inserted in the middle comes out clean.
8. Let cool in the pan for 15 minutes before transferring to a wire rack to cool completely.
9. Dust with powdered sugar before serving.

Nutrition Information:
Calories: 231, Total Fat: 9.7g, Saturated Fat: 5.5g, Cholesterol: 58mg, Sodium: 140mg, Carbohydrates: 33.2g, Fiber: 0.7g, Sugar: 20g, Protein: 4.2g

53. Brown Sugar Pecan Bread

This recipe for Brown Sugar Pecan Bread is a delicious and flavorful bread with a delightful crunch. It's great on its own or as an accompaniment to a cup of tea or coffee. The brown sugar gives it a sweet and slightly caramel-like flavor while the pecans add additional texture and nutty flavor.

Serving: 10 slices | Preparation Time: 20 mins | Ready Time: 55 mins

Ingredients:
- 2 1/4 cups all-purpose flour
- 1 1/3 cups light brown sugar
- 1 teaspoon baking soda
- 1/2 teaspoon salt
- 1 cup chopped pecans
- 2 eggs, lightly beaten
- 1 cup buttermilk
- 1/4 cup vegetable oil

Instructions:
1. Preheat oven to 350° F. Grease and flour a 9x5 inch loaf pan.
2. In a large bowl, whisk together the flour, brown sugar, baking soda, and salt.
3. Add the pecans and mix until evenly distributed.
4. In a separate bowl, mix together the eggs, buttermilk, and vegetable oil.
5. Pour the wet ingredients over the dry ingredients and stir until just combined.
6. Transfer the batter to the loaf pan and bake for 45-55 minutes, or until a toothpick inserted into the center comes out clean.
7. Allow the bread to cool for 10 minutes before transferring to a cooling rack.

Nutrition Information:
Serving Size: 1 slice
Calories: 213 kcal, Fat: 8 g, Carbohydrates: 31 g, Protein: 3 g, Fiber: 1 g, Sugar: 15 g

54. Smoked Gouda Cornbread

This Smoked Gouda Cornbread is a cheesy, savory twist on a classic. The smoked gouda cheese packs a lot of flavor into a light and spongy cornbread. Ideal for a side dish or for a snack, this cornbread recipe is sure to become a favorite!

Serving: 10 – 12 | Preparation Time: 10 min | Ready Time: 40 min

Ingredients:
- 2 cups cornmeal
- 2 cups all-purpose flour
- 1/4 cup sugar
- 2 teaspoons salt
- 2 tablespoons baking soda
- 1/2 cup vegetable oil
- 2 cups buttermilk
- 2 eggs
- 1/2 cup minced red onion
- 4 ounces smoked gouda cheese, shredded
- 1/2 cup fresh corn kernels

Instructions:
1. Preheat the oven to 375F (190°C) and grease a 9-inch round baking dish with butter.
2. In a large bowl, whisk together the cornmeal, flour, sugar, salt, and baking soda.
3. In a medium bowl, whisk together the oil, buttermilk, and eggs.
4. Add the wet ingredients to the dry ingredients, stirring until just combined.
5. Fold in the onion, cheese, and corn.
6. Pour the batter into the prepared baking dish.
7. Bake for 40 minutes, until the top is golden brown and a toothpick inserted into the center comes out clean.
8. Let cool for 10 minutes before slicing and serving.

Nutrition Information:
Per serving: 200 calories, 9.3g fat, 21.3g carbohydrates, 3.7g protein.

55. Rhubarb Bread

Rhubarb Bread is a delicious and flavorful treat, perfect for breakfast, dessert, and snack time. With a slightly tangy yet sweet taste, this bread is sure to be a hit.

Serving: 8. | Preparation Time: 10 minutes | Ready Time: 1 hour.

Ingredients:
- 2 cup all-purpose flour
- 1 cup white sugar
- 1 teaspoon baking powder
- 1 teaspoon baking soda
- 1/2 teaspoon salt
- 1 cup chopped fresh rhubarb
- 1/2 cup butter, softened
- 2 eggs
- 2/3 cup honey

Instructions:
1. Preheat oven to 350F. Grease 8×4 loaf pan.
2. In a large bowl, mix together flour, sugar, baking powder, baking soda, and salt. Add butter, eggs, honey, and rhubarb, stirring until well blended.
3. Pour bread mixture into prepared pan, and bake for about 1 hour until golden brown.

Nutrition Information:
Serving Size: 1 slice, Calories: 225, Fat: 10g, Carbohydrates: 30g, Protein: 4g, Sodium: 280mg, Sugar: 16g.

56. Garlic Herb Bread

This savory Garlic Herb Bread is sure to be a hit with guests and family alike! With a combination of fresh garlic, herbs, and butter, this bread has the perfect flavor combination.

Serving: 4-6 | Preparation Time: 10-15 minutes | Ready Time: 30-35 minutes

Ingredients:
-3 tablespoons of butter, melted
-1 tablespoon of chopped fresh parsley
-1 teaspoon of chopped fresh rosemary

Instructions:
1. Preheat the oven to 375 degrees F.
2. Cut a loaf of French bread lengthwise.
3. In a small bowl, combine the melted butter, chopped parsley, and chopped rosemary.
4. Spread the butter mixture evenly on top of the bread.
5. Bake for 30-35 minutes, until the bread is golden brown.

Nutrition Information:
Per Serving: 130 calories, 8g fat, 18g carbs, 3g protein

57. Date Bread

Date bread is a decadently sweet, moist, rich and delicious bread that is perfect for breakfast, brunch, or dessert. It is a simple treat that is easy to make yet yields amazing results.

Serving: 8-10 slices | Preparation Time: 15 minutes | Ready Time: 1 hour 10 minutes

Ingredients:
- 2 1/2 cups all-purpose flour
- 2 teaspoons baking powder
- 1 teaspoon baking soda
- 1/2 teaspoon salt
- 1/2 cup butter, softened
- 1/2 cup white sugar
- 1/2 cup light brown sugar
- 2 eggs
- 1 1/2 cups dates, chopped
- 1 teaspoon vanilla extract
- 1/2 cup milk

Instructions:
1. Preheat the oven to 350 F (175 °C). Grease a 9x5 inch loaf pan.

2. In a medium bowl, stir together the flour, baking powder, baking soda and salt.

3. In a large bowl, beat together the butter, white sugar, and brown sugar until creamy. Beat in the eggs, one at a time.

4. Stir in the dates and vanilla. Slowly add the dry ingredients, alternating with the milk.

5. Pour the batter into the prepared pan and spread evenly.

6. Bake for about 1 hour, or until the bread is golden brown and a toothpick inserted in the center comes out clean.

Nutrition Information:
Serving size 1 slice (117 grams); Calories 181; Protein 2.8 g; Total fat 7.5 g; Saturated fat 4.5 g; Carbohydrates 25.6 g; Dietary fiber 1.3 g; Sugar 10.7 g; Sodium 132 mg; Potassium 205 mg; Calcium 40 mg; Vitamin A 371 IU; Vitamin C 0.2 mg.

58. Chocolate Zucchini Bread

Chocolate Zucchini Bread is a moist and delicious loaf that combines the goodness of zucchini and the sweetness of chocolate for a savory treat. Perfect for a dessert or snack, this Chocolate Zucchini Bread is simple to make and is sure to please!

Serving: Makes one 9-inch (23 cm) loaf | Preparation Time: 15 minutes | Ready Time: 1 hour

Ingredients:
- 2 cups all-purpose flour
- 1 teaspoon baking soda
- 1/2 teaspoon baking powder
- 1/2 teaspoon salt
- 2 cups shredded zucchini
- 1/4 cup vegetable oil
- 1/4 cup buttermilk
- 2 large eggs
- 3/4 cup granulated sugar
- 1/2 cup semi-sweet chocolate chips

Instructions:
1. Preheat oven to 350F (180°C). Grease a loaf pan with butter or nonstick cooking spray.
2. In a large bowl, whisk flour, baking soda, baking powder and salt together.
3. In a separate bowl, mix zucchini, oil, buttermilk, eggs, and sugar together.
4. Add wet ingredients to flour mixture, stirring until just combined.
5. Fold in chocolate chips.
6. Pour batter into the prepared pan.
7. Bake in preheated oven for 45-50 minutes, or until a toothpick inserted in the center comes out clean.
8. Allow to cool before slicing and serving.

Nutrition Information:
Per slice:calories – 275, fat – 11 g, carbs – 39 g, protein – 4 g

59. Cranberry Honey Bread

Cranberry Honey Bread is a warm and delicious treat made with fresh cranberries and honey. This lightly sweetened bread is perfect for breakfast, brunch, snacks, or even dessert!

Serving: 8 | Preparation Time: 25 minutes | Ready Time: 1 hour 10 minutes

Ingredients:
- 2 cups all-purpose flour
- 2 teaspoons baking powder
- 1 teaspoon baking soda
- 1/2 teaspoon salt
- 1/4 teaspoon cinnamon
- 1/2 cup honey
- 1 cup whole cranberries
- 2 large eggs
- 1/2 cup butter, melted
- 1 cup buttermilk

Instructions:
1. Preheat oven to 350F. Grease a 9x5-inch loaf pan and set aside.
2. In a medium bowl, whisk together the flour, baking powder, baking soda, salt, and cinnamon.
3. In a separate medium bowl, whisk together the honey, cranberries, eggs, butter, and buttermilk until fully combined.
4. Add the wet ingredients to the dry ingredients and stir until just combined. Do not over-mix.
5. Pour the batter into the prepared loaf pan and spread evenly. Bake for 50-60 minutes or until a toothpick inserted into the center comes out clean.
6. Let the bread cool for 10 minutes in the pan before transferring to a wire rack to finish cooling.

Nutrition Information:
130 calories, 2g protein, 17g carbohydrates, 6g fat

60. Mustard Dill Quick Bread

Mustard Dill Quick Bread is a savory and flavorful bread perfect for special occasions. This recipe yields a moist and tender loaf, and is surprisingly easy to prepare. This bread can be served as an appetizer or as an accompaniment to dinner.

Serving: 8 slices | Preparation Time: 10 minutes | Ready Time: 70 minutes

Ingredients:
- 2 cups all-purpose flour
- 1 teaspoon baking soda
- 1 teaspoon salt
- 2 tablespoons yellow mustard
- 1 tablespoon fresh dill, chopped
- 2 large eggs
- 1 cup plain yogurt
- 1/2 cup extra virgin olive oil
- 1/4 cup honey

Instructions:
1. Preheat oven to 350F. Grease a 9 x 5-inch loaf pan and set aside.
2. In a large bowl, whisk together the flour, baking soda and salt.
3. In a medium bowl, mix together the mustard, dill, eggs, yogurt, oil and honey. Stir until combined.
4. Add wet ingredients to the dry ingredients and mix until just combined.
5. Pour batter into the prepared pan and spread into an even layer.
6. Bake for 60-70 minutes, or until a toothpick inserted into the center comes out clean.

Nutrition Information:
Serving size: 1 slice, Calories: 246; Total Fat: 14g; Sodium: 496mg; Total Carbohydrate: 24g; Protein: 5g

61. Chocolate Chip Zucchini Bread

This delicious Chocolate Chip Zucchini Bread is a moist and flavorful bread that combines zucchini, chocolate chips and a hint of nutmeg for the perfect blend of sweet and savory. The added zucchini creates a light, fluffy bread that pairs perfectly with a cup of coffee or a scoop of ice cream.

Serving: 8 | Preparation Time: 10 minutes | Ready Time: 1 hour

Ingredients:
-2 1/2 cups all-purpose flour
-1 teaspoon baking soda
-1/2 teaspoon baking powder
-1/2 teaspoon salt
-1 teaspoon ground nutmeg
-1/2 cup butter, softened
-1 cup white sugar
-2 eggs
-1 teaspoon vanilla extract
-1 cup grated zucchini
-1/2 cup semisweet chocolate chips

Instructions:
1. Preheat oven to 350 degrees F (175 degrees C). Lightly grease a 9x5 inch loaf pan.
2. Combine the flour, baking soda, baking powder, salt and nutmeg in a bowl; set aside.
3. Cream together the butter and sugar until light and fluffy. Beat in the eggs one at a time, then stir in the vanilla.
4. Gradually stir the dry ingredients into the batter. Gently fold in the zucchini and chocolate chips.
5. Pour batter into the prepared pan.
6. Bake for 50 minutes to 1 hour in the preheated oven, or until a toothpick inserted into the center of the bread comes out clean. Cool for 10 minutes in the pan, then turn out onto wire rack to cool completely.

Nutrition Information
Serving size: 1 slice, Calories: 245, Total Fat: 10.3g, Cholesterol: 48.2mg, Sodium: 208.9mg, Total Carbohydrates: 33.6g, Fiber: 1.2g, Protein: 3.2g

62. Banana Raisin Bread

This delicious banana raisin bread is a perfect way to get a warm, sweet and cozy treat that is easy to make.

Serving: 4 | Preparation Time: 10 minutes | Ready Time: 1 hour

Ingredients:
-3 ripe bananas, mashed
-1/3 cup of melted butter
-1/2 cup of sugar

Instructions:
1. Preheat oven to 350F and lightly grease a 9" x 5" loaf pan.
2. In a medium bowl, stir together mashed bananas, melted butter, and sugar.
3. In a separate bowl, mix together the flour, baking soda, and salt.
4. Add the dry ingredients to the wet ingredients until the flour is just incorporated.

5. Pour the batter into the prepared pan and sprinkle the top with the raisins.

6. Bake at 350F for 45-55 minutes or until a knife inserted into the center comes out clean.

7. Let cool in the pan for 10 minutes, then transfer to a rack to cool completely.

Nutrition Information:
158 calories, 8 g fat, 20 g carbohydrates, 1 g protein.

63. Cinnamon Streusel Bread

Cinnamon Streusel Bread is an indulgent and comforting dessertbread. It is a combination of sweet cinnamon and crunchy streusel topping that make for an irresistible combination.

Serving: 10-15 slices | Preparation Time: 20 minutes | Ready Time: 1 hour 10 minutes

Ingredients:
- 2 cups all-purpose flour
- 2 teaspoons baking powder
- 3/4 teaspoon salt
- 2 eggs
- 2/3 cup granulated sugar
- 1/2 cup vegetable oil
- 1/3 cup milk
- 2 tablespoons ground cinnamon
- Streusel topping:(1/2 cup light brown sugar, 1/2 cup all-purpose flour, 1/4 cup butter, 1/4 cup chopped pecans)

Instructions:
1. Preheat oven to 350F. Grease a 9x5 inch loaf pan with butter.
2. In a medium bowl, whisk together the flour, baking powder, and salt. Set aside.
3. In a separate bowl, whisk together the eggs, sugar, vegetable oil and milk.

4. Add the dry ingredients to the wet ingredients and mix until just combined.
5. Pour the batter into the prepared loaf pan.
6. Mix together the cinnamon and streusel topping, then sprinkle it over the top of the batter.
7. Bake for 50 minutes or until a toothpick inserted comes out clean.
8. Let cool before slicing.

Nutrition Information:
Serving Size: 1 slice, Calories: 273, Total Fat: 14g, Saturated Fat: 5g, Cholesterol: 35mg, Sodium: 200mg, Total Carbohydrates: 33g, Dietary Fiber: 1g, Sugars: 17g, Protein: 4g

64. Cherry Almond Bread

Cherry Almond Bread is a sweet, moist streak cake-like bread packed full of juicy cherries and crunchy toasted almonds. It is perfect as a delightful breakfast treat or as an afternoon snack.

Serving: 10-12 slices | Preparation Time: 20 minutes | Ready Time: 1 hour

Ingredients:

-1 3/4 cups all-purpose flour
-1/2 teaspoons of baking powder
-3 tablespoons of sugar
-1 teaspoon almond extract
-2 large eggs
-1/4 cup butter (melted)
-1/2 cup sour cream
-1/3 cup heavy cream
-1 cup pitted cherries
-3 tablespoons sliced or slivered almonds, toasted

Instructions:
1. Preheat oven to 350F. Grease a 9x5 loaf pan.

2. In a medium bowl, whisk together the flour, baking powder, and sugar.
3. In a separate large bowl, whisk together almond extract, eggs, melted butter, sour cream, and heavy cream.
4. Add the dry ingredients to the wet ingredients and stir until just combined.
5. Fold in the cherries, and then pour the batter into the prepared loaf pan.
6. Top with the toasted almonds and bake for 45-55 minutes, or until a toothpick inserted in the center comes out mostly clean.
7. Let cool before removing from the pan and slicing.

Nutrition Information (per serving):
Calories: 220 kcal; Fat: 11 g; Saturated Fat: 5 g; Protein: 4 g; Carbohydrate: 27 g; Sugars: 10 g; Cholesterol: 53 mg; Sodium: 78 mg; Potassium: 107 mg

65. Coconut Pumpkin Bread

Coconut Pumpkin Bread is a delicious autumnal-inspired sweet treat that is the perfect balance of pumpkin spice and coconut flavors. It is ideal for sharing with friends and family and is sure to be a hit.

Serving: 10-12 slices | Preparation Time: 10 minutes | Ready Time: 1 hour

Ingredients:
-3/4 cup all-purpose flour
-3/4 cup whole wheat flour
-1 teaspoon baking powder
-1/2 teaspoon baking soda
-2 teaspoons ground cinnamon
-1/4 teaspoon ground nutmeg
-1/2 teaspoon salt
-1 egg, lightly beaten
-1/2 cup canned pumpkin puree
-1/2 cup coconut oil, melted
-1/2 cup coconut milk

-1/2 cup maple syrup
-2 teaspoons vanilla extract
-1/2 cup sweetened coconut flakes

Instructions:
1. Preheat oven to 350 degrees F and grease a 9x5-inch loaf pan.
2. In a medium bowl, whisk together the flours, baking powder, baking soda, cinnamon, nutmeg, and salt.
3. In a separate bowl, whisk together the egg, pumpkin puree, coconut oil, coconut milk, maple syrup, and vanilla extract.
4. Slowly add the dry ingredients to the wet ingredients and stir until just combined. Do not overmix.
5. Fold in the coconut flakes and stir gently.
6. Pour the batter into the prepared loaf pan and spread evenly.
7. Place in preheated oven and bake for 45-50 minutes or until a toothpick inserted comes out clean.
8. Allow the loaf to cool for 30 minutes before slicing and serving.

Nutrition Information:
Calories: 396 kcal, Carbohydrates: 45.9 g, Protein: 5.1 g, Fat: 22.8 g, Saturated Fat: 16.5 g, Cholesterol: 28.5 mg, Sodium: 248 mg, Potassium: 183 g, Fiber: 3.2 g, Sugar: 28.2 g, Vitamin A: 1000 IU, Vitamin C: 1.1 mg, Calcium: 78 mg, Iron: 2.5 mg

66. Peanut Butter Banana Bread

This Peanut Butter Banana Bread is an easy to make yet delicious and moist sweet bread that is perfect as a snack or dessert! Serving 8-10, it's ready in just under an hour.

Serving: 8-10 | Preparation Time: 15 minutes | Ready Time: 45 minutes

Ingredients:
- 3 medium ripe bananas
- 1/2 cup creamy peanut butter
- 2 eggs
- 2/3 cup sugar
- 1 teaspoon baking soda

- 1/2 teaspoon baking powder
- 1 teaspoon salt
- 1 1/2 cup flour

Instructions:
1. Preheat oven to 350 degrees F (175 degrees C).
2. In a large bowl, mash the ripe bananas together with a fork.
3. Mix in the peanut butter, eggs, sugar, baking soda, baking powder, and salt.
4. Add in the flour, stirring until combined.
5. Grease a 9x5 inch loaf pan and spread the batter evenly.
6. Bake in preheated oven for 40 minutes, or until a toothpick inserted into the center comes out clean.
7. Let cool before serving.

Nutrition Information:
Calories: 343, Fat: 12.5g, Saturated fat: 2.6g, Carbohydrates: 52.6g, Sugar: 27.2g, Sodium: 355mg, Fiber: 2.5g, Protein: 9.1g

67. Sweet Potato Chocolate Chip Bread

Introducing Sweet Potato Chocolate Chip Bread—a delicious and healthy dessert option perfect for any kind of special occasion! This flavorful bread is soft and moist, filled with melted chocolate chips and sweet potato. Serve it up to your guests with a scoop of ice cream or a dollop of yogurt for the perfect end to a great meal.

Serving: 12-14 pieces | Preparation Time: 20min | Ready Time: 1h15min

Ingredients:
-2 cups all purpose flour
-1 teaspoon baking powder
-1/2 teaspoon baking soda
-1/2 teaspoon salt
-1 teaspoon cinnamon
-3/4 cup melted butter
-3/4 cup brown sugar
-2 eggs

-1 teaspoon vanilla
-1 cup mashed sweet potato
-1/2 cup semi-sweet chocolate chips

Instructions:
1. Preheat oven to 350F and then grease and flour a 9-inch loaf pan.
2. In a medium bowl, whisk together the flour, baking powder, baking soda, salt, and cinnamon. Set aside.
3. In a large bowl, cream together the melted butter and brown sugar until light and fluffy.
4. Beat in the eggs into the butter-sugar mixture, one at a time, followed by the vanilla.
5. Stir in the mashed sweet potato until fully incorporated and then slowly add the dry ingredients, stirring until everything is evenly distributed.
6. Finally fold in the chocolate chips and pour the batter into the prepared loaf pan.
7. Bake for 1 hour and 15minutes, or until a toothpick inserted into the center of the loaf comes out clean.

Nutrition Information:
Serving Size: 1 slice, Calories: 220, Fat: 8.3g, Carbohydrates: 32.2g, Protein: 3.2g

68. Date Pecan Bread

Date Pecan Bread is a delicious, sweet and spiced one-bowl quick bread recipe that is created with the unique combination of dates, pecans and sugar. It perfect for serving with tea or coffee, as a mid-day snack or as an after-dinner dessert.

Serving: 12 | Preparation Time: 15 minutes | Ready Time: 55 minutes

Ingredients:
- 2 cups all-purpose flour
- 2 teaspoons baking powder
- 1/2 teaspoon salt
- 1/2 cup chopped cashews

- 1/2 cup chopped dates
- 1/2 cup chopped pecans
- 2/3 cup brown sugar
- 2 eggs
- 1/4 cup vegetable oil
- 2/3 cup milk

Instructions:
1. Preheat oven to 350F/175C. Grease 9x5-inch loaf pan and set aside.
2. In a large mixing bowl, whisk together flour, baking powder and salt until combined.
3. Add cashews, dates and pecans, and toss until evenly combined. Stir in brown sugar.
4. In a separate bowl, whisk together eggs, oil and milk until combined.
5. Pour wet ingredients into the dry mixture and stir until just combined.
6. Pour the batter into prepared pan and bake for 45-55 minutes or until a toothpick inserted in the center comes out clean.
7. Cool the bread in the pan for 10 minutes before transferring it to a cooling rack.

Nutrition Information (per serving):
Calories 296; Total Fat 11g; Saturated Fat 2.9g; Cholesterol 33mg; Sodium 161mg; Total Carbohydrate 44g; Dietary Fiber 2.3g; Protein 5.9g

69. Apple Streusel Bread

Apple Streusel Bread is a moist and delicious sweet treat, laced with warm cinnamon and plenty of juicy apples. This quick and easy-to-make loaf is the perfect way to bring the cozy flavor of fall into your kitchen.

Serving: 1 loaf | Preparation Time: 15 minutes | Ready Time: 1 hour 10 minutes

Ingredients:
-3 cups all-purpose flour
-2 teaspoons baking powder
-1/2 teaspoon baking soda

-1 teaspoon ground cinnamon
-1/2 teaspoon salt
-3 eggs
-1/2 cup vegetable oil
-1 cup white sugar
-1 teaspoon vanilla extract
-1 cup buttermilk
-2 apples, peeled, cored, and diced
-1/2 cup brown sugar
-1 teaspoon ground cinnamon
-4 tablespoons cold butter, cut into cubes

Instructions:
1. Preheat oven to 350 degrees F (175 degrees C). Grease a 9x5-inch loaf pan.
2. In a medium bowl, stir together the flour, baking powder, baking soda, 1 teaspoon cinnamon, and salt.
3. In a large bowl, beat together eggs, oil, sugar, and vanilla. Gradually beat in the dry ingredients, and then the buttermilk. Fold in the apples.
4. In a small bowl, stir together the brown sugar, 1 teaspoon cinnamon, and butter until crumbly.
5. Pour the batter into prepared loaf pan. Sprinkle streusel topping over the top.
6. Bake in preheated oven for 55 to 60 minutes, or until a toothpick inserted into the loaf comes out clean.

Nutrition Information:
Calories: 250; Total Fat: 9.9g; Cholesterol: 43.6mg; Sodium: 333mg; Total Carbohydrate: 36.1g; Protein: 4.3g; Potassium: 174mg

70. Carrot Cake

Carrot Cake is a classic that you and your family will love! With its soft, flavorful cake and creamy cream cheese frosting, this classic dessert is just as delicious as it is beautiful. Serving 8-10, this Carrot Cake can be prepared in 45 minutes and is ready to be enjoyed in 1 hour.

Serving: 8-10 | Preparation Time: 45 minutes | Ready Time: 1 hour

Ingredients:
- 2 cups all-purpose flour
- 2 teaspoons baking soda
- 2 teaspoons ground cinnamon
- 1 teaspoon salt
- 4 eggs
- 1 cup vegetable oil
- 2 cups white sugar
- 3 cups grated carrots
- 1 teaspoon vanilla extract
  1/2 cup chopped walnuts (optional)

Instructions:
1. Preheat the oven to 350 degrees F (175 degrees C).
2. Grease and flour a 9x13 inch pan.
3. In a medium bowl, combine together flour, baking soda, cinnamon and salt.
4. In a large bowl, beat eggs until light and foamy. Add oil and sugar, and beat until well blended. Add the dry ingredients to the wet ingredients, and mix until just combined. Stir in carrots, vanilla, and nuts if desired.
5. Pour the batter into the prepared pan and spread evenly.
6. Bake in preheated oven for 35 to 40 minutes, or until a toothpick inserted in the center of the cake comes out clean.
7. Allow cake to cool in pan before frosting.

Nutrition Information:
Each slice of Carrot Cake contains 468 calories, 20.7g of fat, 67.8g of carbohydrates and 5.5g of protein.

71. Chocolate Peanut Butter Bread

Chocolate Peanut Butter Bread is a delicious, hearty, and rich twist on classic peanut butter and jelly. This beautiful and flavourful bread is a perfect accompaniment to any picnic or meal!

Serving: 8 | Preparation Time: 20 minutes | Ready Time: 2 hours

Ingredients:

- 2 1/2 cups all-purpose flour
- 1/4 cup cocoa powder
- 1 teaspoon baking powder
- 1/2 teaspoon baking soda
- 1/2 teaspoon salt
- 3/4 cup creamy peanut butter
- 2/3 cup sugar
- 1/4 cup light brown sugar
- 2 large eggs
- 2 teaspoons pure vanilla extract
- 1 cup of whole milk

Instructions:

1. Preheat oven to 350 degrees F. Grease a 9x5-inch loaf pan and dust it with cocoa powder.
2. In a medium bowl, whisk together the flour, cocoa powder, baking powder, baking soda and salt.
3. In the bowl of an electric mixer, beat together the peanut butter and sugars until light and fluffy.
4. Add in the eggs one at a time, and mix until well combined.
5. Stir in the vanilla extract.
6 Alternate between adding in the dry ingredients and the milk, mixing until everything is just evenly combined.
7. Pour the batter into the prepared pan and spread it evenly.
8. Bake for 45 minutes to 1 hour, or until a toothpick inserted in the center of the bread comes out clean.
9. Cool in the pan for 15 minutes before turning it out onto a cooling rack.

Nutrition Information:

Serving Size 1 slice; Calories 340; Fat 10 g; Saturated Fat 2 g; Carbohydrates 54 g; Sugar 18g; Protein 9 g; Fiber 2 g; Cholesterol 38 mg; Sodium 420 mg.

72. Honey Oat Bread

Honey Oat Bread is a hearty, delicious, and sweet bread that is perfect toasted and served with butter or jam. This easy-to-make loaf is sure to quickly become a family favorite.

Serving: 2 Loaves | Preparation Time: 10 minutes | Ready Time: 1 hour and 25 minutes

Ingredients:
- 2 cups wheat flour
- 1/2 teaspoon salt
- 1/2 cup oats
- 2 tablespoons honey
- 1 tablespoon vegetable oil
- 2 teaspoons active dry yeast
- 1 1/4 cups warm water

Instructions:
1. In a bowl, mix together the wheat flour, salt, oats, honey, and vegetable oil.
2. Dissolve the yeast in the warm water and pour into the dry ingredients. Stir until a dough is formed.
3. Turn the dough onto a lightly floured surface and knead for about 10 minutes or until the dough is smooth.
4. Place the dough in an oiled bowl, cover and let rise in a warm place until doubled in size, about 45 minutes.
5. Punch the dough down and form into a loaf. Place in a greased 8x4 inch loaf pan. Cover it and let it rise in a warm place until doubled in size, about 30 minutes.
6. Preheat the oven to 375F (190°C).
7. Bake the loaf in the oven for 25 minutes or until golden brown.
8. Cool in the pan for 10 minutes before removing and cooling completely on a wire rack.

Nutrition Information:
Calories: 210, Fat: 4.3g, Carbohydrates: 39.3g, Protein: 5.9g

73. Cheddar Cornbread

Cheddar Cornbread is a cheesy, savory twist on classic cornbread. It's an easy preparation and great for pairing with stew or chili.

Serving: 6-8 slices | Preparation Time: 10 minutes | Ready Time: 30 minutes

Ingredients:
- 1 cup all-purpose flour
- 1 cup corn meal
- 2 teaspoons baking powder
- 1 teaspoon salt
- 2 tablespoons sugar
- 1/2 cup butter, melted
- 1 large egg
- 1 cup buttermilk
- 1 cup shredded cheddar cheese

Instructions:
1. Preheat oven to 400 degrees F. Grease a 9-inch round pan with butter.
2. In a large bowl, mix together the flour, cornmeal, baking powder, salt and sugar.
3. In a small bowl, mix together the melted butter, egg and buttermilk, then pour into the flour mixture.
4. Gently fold in the shredded cheddar cheese.
5. Pour batter into the greased pan, and spread evenly with a spatula.
6. Bake for 20 to 30 minutes or until golden brown.

Nutrition Information:
Calories: 263, Protein: 5g, Total Fat: 14g, Cholesterol: 44mg, Sodium: 449mg, Carbohydrates: 25g, Fiber: 2g

74. Walnut Chocolate Chip Bread

This Walnut Chocolate Chip Bread is a delicious and moist treat that tastes almost like dessert. With a combination of crunchy walnuts and soft, chocolate chips, this bread is sure to delight the taste buds. Serve warm or at room temperature with a generous serving of butter.

Serving: 8 | Preparation Time: 10 minutes | Ready Time: 45 minutes

Ingredients:
- 2 cups all-purpose flour
- 1 teaspoon baking powder
- 1 teaspoon baking soda
- 1/2 teaspoon salt
- 1/2 cup butter, softened
- 1 cup granulated sugar
- 2 large eggs
- 1 teaspoon vanilla extract
- 1 cup buttermilk
- 1 cup coarsely chopped walnuts
- 1 cup semisweet chocolate chips

Instructions:
1. Preheat oven to 350F (176C). Grease a 9x5-inch loaf pan.
2. In a large bowl, mix together the flour, baking powder, baking soda, and salt.
3. In a separate bowl, cream together the butter and sugar until light and fluffy. Beat in the eggs and vanilla until combined.
4. Gradually add the dry ingredients to the butter mixture, alternating with the buttermilk and stirring after each addition.
5. Fold in the walnuts and chocolate chips until fully incorporated.
6. Pour the batter into the prepared pan and spread evenly. Bake for 40 to 45 minutes, or until a toothpick comes out clean from the center. Let cool in the pan for 10 minutes before transferring it to a wire rack to cool completely.

Nutrition Information:
Serving Size 1 slice
Calories 367 calories, Carbohydrates 43 g, Protein 6 g, Fat 19 g, Saturated Fat 10 g, Cholesterol 48 mg, Sodium 384 mg, Potassium 131 mg, Fiber 2 g, Sugar 23 g, Vitamin A 386 IU, Vitamin C 1 mg, Calcium 69 mg, Iron 1 mg

75. Chocolate Chip Grape Bread

Chocolate Chip Grape Breadis a delicious sweet treat that is sure to be a favorite with everyone. With the combination of dark chocolate and sweet grapes, this quick bread is a special treat for any occasion!

Serving: Makes 8-10 slices | Preparation Time: 10 minutes | Ready Time: 1 hour and 10 minutes

Ingredients:
-2 cups all purpose flour
-1 teaspoon baking powder
-1/2 teaspoon baking soda
-3/4 teaspoon salt
-5 tablespoons butter, softened
-2/3 cup brown sugar
-2 large eggs
-2 teaspoons vanilla extract
-1 cup dark chocolate chunks
-1 cup seedless red grapes, chopped

Instructions:
1. Preheat oven to 350°F and line a 9"x5" loaf pan with parchment paper.
2. In a medium bowl, sift together the flour, baking powder, baking soda, and salt.
3. In a large bowl, cream together the butter and brown sugar until light and fluffy.
4. Beat in the eggs, one at a time.
5. Add the vanilla extract and mix until just combined.
6. Slowly add in the flour mixture and mix on low speed until just combined.
7. Stir in the chocolate chunks and grapes.
8. Pour the batter into the prepared loaf pan and bake for 45-50 minutes, or until a toothpick inserted into the center comes out clean.
9. Allow to cool before slicing and serving.

Nutrition Information:
Per slice: Calories: 377, Fat: 15g, Carbs: 51g, Protein: 6g

76. Applesauce Spice Cake

This Applesauce Spice Cake is a delicious combination of applesauce, warm spices and other tasty ingredients. With a moist and crumbly texture and a subtle sweetness, this cake is sure to be a hit with family and friends!

Serving: 12 slices | Preparation Time: 30 minutes | Ready Time: 1 hour

Ingredients:
- 2 cups all-purpose flour
- 2 teaspoons baking powder
- 1 teaspoon ground cinnamon
- 1/2 teaspoon ground nutmeg
- 1/2 teaspoon ground ginger
- 1/4 teaspoon ground allspice
- 1/4 cup (1/2 stick) butter or margarine, at room temperature
- 3/4 cup granulated sugar
- 2 eggs
- 1/2 cup applesauce
- 2 tablespoons brandy or apple juice

Instructions:
1. Preheat oven to 350F. Grease and flour an 8-inch-square baking pan.
2. In a medium bowl, sift together flour, baking powder, cinnamon, nutmeg, ginger and allspice; set aside.
3. In a large bowl, cream together butter and sugar until light and fluffy. Beat in eggs one at a time, then stir in applesauce and brandy.
4. Gradually add flour mixture to butter mixture, stirring until just combined.
5. Spread batter evenly into prepared pan. Bake for 30 to 35 minutes, or until a toothpick inserted into the center of the cake comes out clean.
6. Cool cake in pan on wire rack for 10 minutes, then turn out onto wire rack to cool completely.

Nutrition Information:

Per serving: 188 calories, 8 g fat (5 g saturated fat), 43 mg cholesterol, 94 mg sodium, 27 g carbohydrate, 1 g dietary fiber, 16 g sugar, 3 g protein.

77. Maple Walnut Banana Bread

This Maple Walnut Banana Bread is a moist and flavorful banana bread that adds a delicious twist with the maple and crunchy walnuts. It is sure to quickly become a family favorite!

Serving: 12 | Preparation Time: 10 minutes | Ready Time: 55 minutes

Ingredients:
- 2 tablespoons of maple syrup
- 1/2 cup of softened butter
- 2 large ripe bananas
- 2 eggs
- 1 teaspoon of baking soda
- 1/2 teaspoon of baking powder
- 2 cups of all-purpose flour
- 1/3 cup of chopped walnuts

Instructions:
1. Preheat oven to 375F and lightly grease an 8x4-inch loaf pan with butter.
2. In a large bowl, cream together butter and maple syrup until light and fluffy.
3. Mash the ripe bananas and add them to the butter mixture. Beat in the eggs until well blended.
4. In a separate bowl, combine baking soda, baking powder, and all-purpose flour. Gradually add the dry ingredients to the butter mixture, stirring until everything is blended together.
5. Gently stir in the chopped walnuts.
6. Pour the mixture into the prepared pan.
7. Bake for 45 to 55 minutes, or until a toothpick inserted into the center comes out clean.

Nutrition Information:

Calories: 185 kcal; Protein: 4 g; Fat: 10 g; Sodium: 105 mg; Carbohydrates: 22 g; Sugar: 7 g.

78. Blueberry Lemon Pound Cake

This delicious blueberry lemon pound cake is bursting with tart and sweet flavors, as well as a moist, dense texture. It's the perfect way to enjoy a spring or summer day!

Serving: 8-10 | Preparation Time: 15 minutes | Ready Time: 1 hour 10 minutes

Ingredients:
- 2 cups all-purpose flour
- 2 teaspoons baking powder
- 1 teaspoon salt
- 1 cup (2 sticks) butter, at room temperature
- 1 cup granulated sugar
- 3 large eggs
- 1 teaspoon vanilla extract
- 3 tablespoons fresh lemon juice
- 2 cups fresh blueberries

Instructions:
1. Preheat oven to 350°F. Grease a 9-inch loaf pan, then line the bottom and two sides with parchment paper.
2. In a medium bowl, whisk together the flour, baking powder and salt. In a separate large bowl, cream together the butter and sugar until light and fluffy.
3. Beat in the eggs one at a time, mixing until each one is incorporated before adding the next. Stir in the vanilla extract and lemon juice.
4. Slowly add the flour mixture to the wet ingredients, stirring as you go. Once everything is combined, fold in blueberries.
5. Transfer the batter to the prepared loaf pan and bake for 1 hour to 1 hour 10 minutes, until the top is golden brown and a toothpick inserted into the center comes out clean. Let cool before removing from the pan.

Nutrition Information:
Per Serving (based on 10 serving): 287 calories, 16g fat, 36g carbs, 2.4g protein, 4g fiber

79. Apple Pecan Bread

Apple Pecan Bread is a moist and delicious cake-like bread that is packed with sweet and nutty flavors. It is a great addition to any breakfast and snack table.

Serving: 8 | Preparation Time: 10 minutes | Ready Time: 1 hour

Ingredients:
- 2 1/2 cups all-purpose flour
- 1 teaspoon baking soda
- 1 teaspoon ground cinnamon
- 1/4 teaspoon ground nutmeg
- 1/2 teaspoon salt
- 1 cup butter, melted
- 3/4 cup white sugar
- 1/2 cup brown sugar
- 2 large eggs
- 3/4 cup apple juice
- 1 teaspoon vanilla extract
- 2 cups diced apples
- 1 cup chopped pecans

Instructions:
1. Preheat the oven to 350 degrees F and lightly grease a 9x5-inch loaf pan.
2. In a medium bowl, whisk together the flour, baking soda, cinnamon, nutmeg, and salt.
3. In a large bowl, stir together the melted butter and sugars until combined. Beat in the eggs, apple juice, and vanilla until light and fluffy.
4. Slowly add the dry ingredients to the wet ingredients, stirring until just combined. Gently fold in the apples and pecans.
5. Pour the batter into the prepared pan and bake for 40 to 50 minutes, or until a toothpick inserted in the center comes out clean.

6. Allow the loaf to cool in the pan for 15 minutes before transferring to a wire rack to cool completely.

Nutrition Information:
Per Serving (1/8 of the loaf) - Calories: 293, Fat: 13g, Saturated Fat: 7g, Cholesterol: 55mg, Sodium: 202mg, Carbohydrates: 42g, Fiber: 2g, Sugar: 24g, Protein: 4g

80. Pumpkin Streusel Bread

This delectable Pumpkin Streusel Bread is a tasty combination of flavors, with a moist pumpkin and spice cake, topped with an oat streusel crumb topping – it's the perfect way to enjoy the cozy flavors of fall.

Serving: 12-15 | Preparation Time: 15 minutes | Ready Time: 1 hour

Ingredients:
- 2 cups all-purpose flour
- 2 teaspoons baking powder
- 1 teaspoon baking soda
- 1 teaspoon ground cinnamon
- 1/2 teaspoon ground nutmeg
- 1/2 teaspoon ground cloves
- 1/2 teaspoon ground ginger
- 1/4 teaspoon salt
- 1 cup pure pumpkin puree
- 3/4 cup light brown sugar
- 1/4 cup pure maple syrup
- 2 large eggs
- 1/4 cup canola oil
- For the streusel topping:
- 3/4 cup old fashioned rolled oats
- 1/4 cup all-purpose flour
- 2 tablespoons light brown sugar
- 2 tablespoons cold butter

Instructions
1. Preheat oven to 350 degrees F and grease a 9x5-inch loaf pan.
2. In a medium bowl, whisk together the flour, baking powder, baking soda, cinnamon, nutmeg, cloves, ginger and salt.
3. In a large bowl, whisk together the pumpkin puree, brown sugar, maple syrup, eggs and canola oil until combined.
4. Add the dry ingredients to the wet ingredients and gently stir until just combined.
5. Pour the batter into the prepared pan.
6. To make the streusel topping: In a medium bowl, combine the oats, flour and brown sugar. Cut in the cold butter using a pastry blender or your hands, until the mixture is crumbly. Sprinkle the topping over the batter.
7. Bake for 50-60 minutes, or until a toothpick inserted into the center comes out clean.

Nutrition Information: (per 1 slice)
Calories: 184 kcal, Carbs:28 g, Protein:3 g, Fat:7 g

81. Cranberry Orange Pound Cake

This zesty Cranberry Orange Pound Cake is moist and full of flavor. Fresh cranberries and orange juice give the pound cake a delicious citrus kick.

Serving: 8-10 | Preparation Time: 20 minutes | Ready Time: 1 hour and 10 minutes

Ingredients:
- 1/2 cup unsalted butter, room temperature
- 1 1/4 cups granulated sugar
- 2 eggs
- Zest of 2 oranges
- Zest of 2 lemons
- 1 teaspoon pure vanilla extract
- 1 1/2 cups all-purpose flour
- 2 teaspoons baking powder
- 1/2 teaspoon salt

- 1/2 cup orange juice
- 8 ounces fresh cranberries

Instructions:
1. Preheat oven to 350 degrees F and grease a 9-inch bundt pan.
2. In a large bowl, cream together butter and sugar until light and fluffy.
3. Add eggs one at a time, beating well after each addition.
4. Add orange zest, lemon zest, and vanilla extract and mix.
5. In a separate bowl, combine flour, baking powder, and salt.
6. Add dry ingredients gradually to the butter/sugar mixture, alternating with orange juice.
7. Fold in cranberries.
8. Pour batter into prepared pan and bake for 45-50 minutes or until a toothpick inserted into center comes out clean.
9. Allow to cool before serving.

Nutrition Information:
Per Serving:
Calories: 265, Carbohydrates: 39 g, Protein: 4 g, Fat: 10 g, Saturated Fat: 6 g, Cholesterol: 56 mg, Sodium: 189 mg, Fiber: 2 g, Sugar: 23 g

82. Butterscotch Bread

Butterscotch Bread is a delicious, moist, and sweet homemade quick bread. This vegan, nut-free recipe, is perfect for breakfast or as a dessert.

Serving: 10 | Preparation Time: 15 minutes | Ready Time: 60 minutes

Ingredients:
- 2 cups all-purpose flour
- 2 teaspoons baking powder
- 1 teaspoon baking soda
- 1/4 teaspoon salt
- 1 cup butterscotch chips
- 2 tablespoons vegan butter, melted
- 1 cup plant-based milk
- 1/2 cup granulated sugar
- 1/4 cup dark brown sugar

- 1 teaspoon pure vanilla extract

Instructions:
1. Preheat oven to 350 degrees Fahrenheit and line a standard loaf pan with parchment paper.
2. In a medium bowl, whisk together flour, baking powder, baking soda, and salt.
3. In a separate large bowl, whisk together melted butter, milk, sugars, and vanilla extract.
4. Now add the dry ingredients to the wet ingredients, and stir until incorporated.
5. Gently fold in the butterscotch chips, then pour the batter into the prepared loaf pan.
6. Bake for 55-60 minutes, or until a toothpick inserted into the center comes out clean.
7. Let cool in the pan for 10 minutes, then remove and cool completely before slicing.

Nutrition Information:
Calories - 175 kcal, Fat - 6 g, Protein - 2 g, Carbs - 27 g, Fiber - 1 g, Sugar - 14 g, Sodium - 124 mg

83. Peach Pecan Bread

This Peach Pecan Bread is packed with delicious summer flavor, and it's always a hit. Bursting with juicy peaches and crunchy pecans, it's perfect for breakfast, brunch, or an afternoon snack!

Serving: 10 | Preparation Time: 20 minutes | Ready Time: 40 minutes

Ingredients:
- 2 1/2 cups all-purpose flour
- 2 teaspoons baking powder
- 1 teaspoon ground cinnamon
- 1/2 teaspoon baking soda
- 1/4 teaspoon salt
- 2 eggs
- 1 cup granulated sugar

- 1/2 cup vegetable oil
- 2 teaspoons vanilla extract
- 1 can (15oz) sliced peaches, drained
- 3/4 cup pecans, chopped

Instructions:
1. Preheat the oven to 350F and grease a 9x5 baking pan.
2. In a medium bowl, stir together the flour, baking powder, cinnamon, baking soda, and salt.
3. In a separate large bowl, mix together the eggs, sugar, oil, and vanilla.
4. Add the dry ingredients to the wet ingredients and mix until just combined.
5. Gently fold in the drained peaches and chopped pecans.
6. Pour the batter into the prepared baking pan and spread it evenly.
7. Bake for 40-45 minutes, or until a toothpick inserted into the center comes out clean.
8. Let the bread cool completely before slicing.

Nutrition Information:
Calories: 213, Fat: 9g, Cholesterol: 29mg, Sodium: 86mg, Carbohydrates: 30g, Protein: 3g, Fiber: 2g.

84. Cinnamon Apple Bread

This sweet and flavorful Cinnamon Apple Bread is the perfect fall treat. With its delicious combination of fresh apples and warm cinnamon, it's a comfort food classic.

Serving: 8 | Preparation Time: 20 minutes | Ready Time: 1 hour

Ingredients:
- 2 cups of all-purpose flour
- 1 teaspoon of baking soda
- 1 teaspoon of baking powder
- 1/2 teaspoon of salt
- 2 teaspoons of ground cinnamon
- 3/4 cup of sugar
- 2 eggs

- 1/2 cup of vegetable oil
- 1 teaspoon of vanilla extract
- 1 cup of grated apples
- 1/2 cup of chopped walnuts (optional)

Instructions:
1. Preheat oven to 350F (175C). Grease a 9x5 inch loaf pan with butter and dust lightly with flour.
2. In a large bowl, whisk together flour, baking soda, baking powder, salt, and cinnamon.
3. In a separate bowl, beat together the sugar, eggs, oil, and vanilla extract until fully combined.
4. Pour the wet ingredients into the dry ingredients and mix until just combined. Do not over mix.
5. Fold in the grated apple and walnuts.
6. Pour the mixture into the prepared pan and bake for 50-60 minutes, or until a toothpick inserted in the center comes out clean.
7. Let cool before slicing and serving.

Nutrition Information:
Calories: 246, Protein: 4g, Fat: 11g, Carbohydrates: 35g, Dietary Fiber: 2g, Sugar: 18g, Sodium: 246mg

85. Cream Cheese Swirl Bread

Cream Cheese Swirl Bread is a soft, sweet bread that is full of delicious cream cheese swirls! This delicious bread has a soft, fluffy texture and a unique, sweet flavor. The cream cheese swirls add an extra level of creaminess and delightful sweetness. This bread is a perfect accompaniment to any meal and is easy to make!

Serving: 10 | Preparation Time: 15 minutes | Ready Time: 1 hour, 15 minutes

Ingredients:
- 2.5 cups all-purpose flour
- 1 teaspoon salt
- 2 Tablespoons granulated sugar

- 2 Tablespoons vegetable oil
- 1 package active dry yeast
- 1 cup warm water
- 4 ounces cream cheese, softened
- 2 Tablespoons melted butter

Instructions:
1. In a large bowl, whisk together flour, salt, sugar, and oil.
2. In a small bowl, dissolve yeast in warm water. Allow to sit for 5 minutes.
3. Pour yeast mixture into the flour mixture. Using a wooden spoon, mix until just combined.
4. Turn the dough out onto a lightly floured surface and knead until it forms a soft and elastic ball, about 8 minutes. Place the dough ball into a lightly greased bowl and cover with a towel.
5. Allow dough to rise for about 1 hour, or until it doubles in size.
6. In a small bowl, mix together cream cheese and melted butter and set aside.
7. When dough has finished rising, turn it out onto a lightly floured surface, punch it down, and roll it into a large rectangle, about 1/4 inch thick.
8. Spread the cream cheese mixture over the surface of the dough. Starting from the long side, tightly roll the dough into a log. Pinch the seams together. Place in a lightly greased baking pan.
9. Bake in a preheated 350F oven for 40 minutes, or until bread is golden brown. Cool in the pan for 10 minutes before slicing.

Nutrition Information:
1 slice (85g) contains 190 calories, 7.5g fat, 24g carbohydrates, 3.5g sugar, and 4g protein.

86. Maple Carrot Bread

This recipe for Maple Carrot Bread will be sure to have your family and friends asking for more. It is a delicious combination of carrots, maple syrup and walnuts that creates a soft and fluffy bread. Serve this up as a snack or as dessert.

Serving: 8-10 slices | Preparation Time: 10 minutes | Ready Time: 55 minutes

Ingredients:

- 2 eggs
- 2 tablespoons of maple syrup
- 1 teaspoon of vanilla extract
- 3/4 cups of vegetable oil
- 1/2 cup of white sugar
- 1/2 cup of brown sugar
- 1 1/2 cups of grated carrots
- 2 cups of all purpose flour
- 1 teaspoon of baking powder
- 1 teaspoon of baking soda
- 1 teaspoon of ground cinnamon
- 1/2 teaspoon of salt
- 1/2 cup of chopped walnuts

Instructions:

1. Preheat oven to 350 degrees F.
2. In a large bowl, whisk together eggs, maple syrup, vanilla and oil until blended.
3. Stir in both the white and brown sugar, mixing well.
4. Mix in grated carrots.
5. In a separate bowl, whisk together flour, baking powder, baking soda, cinnamon and salt; add to egg mixture and stir until combined.
6. Stir in the chopped nuts.
7. Pour batter into a greased 9x5 inch loaf pan.
8. Bake at 350 degrees F for 45-50 minutes, or until a toothpick inserted into the center comes out clean.

Nutrition Information:

Per Serving (1 slice): Calories: 288, Total Fat: 17 g , Saturated Fat: 3 g, Sodium: 225 mg, Carbohydrates: 31 g, Sugars: 16 g, Protein: 4 g

87. Coconut Blueberry Bread

This delicious Coconut Blueberry Bread is a unique take on a classic treat. Perfectly sweetened with just the right amount of coconut and blueberries, this bread is sure to be a favorite for the whole family.

Serving: Makes 1 loaf | Preparation Time: 15 minutes | Ready Time: 1 hour

Ingredients:
- 2 cups all-purpose flour
- 1/2 teaspoon salt
- 1/2 teaspoon baking powder
- 1/2 teaspoon baking soda
- 3/4 cup coconut flakes
- 3/4 cup frozen blueberries
- 1/4 cup melted butter
- 1/4 cup vegetable oil
- 1 cup white sugar
- 2 eggs
- 2 teaspoons vanilla extract
- 1/2 cup buttermilk

Instructions:
1. Preheat oven to 350 degrees F (175 degrees C). Grease and flour one 9x5 inch loaf pan.
2. Sift together the flour, salt, baking soda, and baking powder.
3. In a separate bowl, cream together the butter, oil, and sugar until smooth. Beat in the eggs one at a time. Stir in the vanilla.
4. Combine the coconut and blueberries with the flour mixture. Alternate between adding the wet ingredients and the flour mixture to the creamed mixture.
5. Pour the batter into the greased loaf pan.
6. Bake at 350 degrees F (175 degrees C). for 65 to 70 minutes, or until a toothpick inserted into the center of the bread comes out clean.

Nutrition Information:
Calories: 346, Fat: 15.7g, Cholesterol: 43mg, Sodium: 207mg, Potassium: 61mg,Carbohydrates: 47.1g, Protein: 3.5g, Fiber 1.5g.

88. Lemon Ricotta Bread

This delicious Lemon Ricotta Bread is a sweet, moist, and refreshing treat! Perfect for breakfast or dessert, this recipe is sure to become a family favorite.

Serving: 10 slices | Preparation Time: 15 minutes | Ready Time: 60 minutes

Ingredients:
-1 1/2 cups ricotta cheese
-2 eggs
-1/2 cup granulated sugar
-1/2 cup vegetable oil
-2 teaspoons grated lemon zest
-2 tablespoons freshly squeezed lemon juice
-1 1/2 cups all-purpose flour
-2 teaspoons baking powder
-1/2 teaspoon baking soda
-1/2 teaspoon salt

Instructions:
1. Preheat oven to 350° F. Grease a 9x5 inch loaf pan with cooking spray and set aside.
2. In a large bowl, beat together the ricotta, eggs, sugar, and oil until well combined. Add in the lemon zest, juice, flour, baking powder, baking soda, and salt and mix until just combined.
3. Pour the batter into the prepared loaf pan and bake for 50-60 minutes, or until an inserted toothpick comes out clean. Let cool before slicing and serving.

Nutrition Information (Per Serving):
Calories 207, Total Fat 12g, Saturated Fat 4g, Cholesterol 40mg, Sodium 204mg, Carbohydrates 19g, Fiber 1g, Sugar 8g, Protein 4g.

89. Cranberry Nut Quick Bread

Cranberry Nut Quick Bread is a delicious and easy quick bread recipe that packs plenty of flavor. Bursting with tart cranberries and crunchy walnuts, it makes a great snack or dessert. This quick bread is ready in just over an hour, so you can quickly bake up something sweet and rewarding.

Serving: 8-10 slices | Preparation Time: 15 minutes | Ready in: 1 hour and 15 minutes

Ingredients:

- 2 cups all-purpose flour
- 2 teaspoons baking powder
- 1/2 teaspoon baking soda
- 1/2 teaspoon salt
- 1/2 cup butter, softened
- 3/4 cup white sugar
- 2 eggs
- 1 teaspoon vanilla extract
- 1/4 cup orange juice
- 2 cups fresh cranberries
- 1/2 cup chopped walnuts

Instructions:

1. Preheat oven to 350F (175°C), and lightly grease a 9x5 inch loaf pan.
2. In a bowl, mix together the flour, baking powder, baking soda and salt.
3. In a separate bowl, cream together the butter and sugar. Beat in the eggs one at a time, then stir in the vanilla and orange juice.
4. Gradually stir the dry ingredients into the wet mixture until everything is just combined. Fold in cranberries and nuts.
5. Spread evenly into the prepared loaf pan.
6. Bake for 55 minutes to 1 hour at 350F (175°C), or until a toothpick inserted into the center of the loaf comes out clean.
7. Allow to cool before slicing.

Nutrition Information:

Calories: 261 kcal, Carbohydrates: 38 g, Protein: 4 g, Fat: 10 g, Saturated Fat: 4 g, Cholesterol: 44 mg, Sodium: 192 mg, Potassium: 123 mg, Fiber: 2 g, Sugar: 21 g, Vitamin A: 202 IU, Vitamin C: 1 mg, Calcium: 64 mg, Iron: 1 mg.

90. Mocha Chocolate Chip Bread

Introducing Mocha Chocolate Chip Bread— a soft, dense, and sweet quick bread with a hint of coffee and melting chocolate chips. A delicious treat that is sure to be a hit among family and friends!

Serving: Makes one 9x5-inch loaf | Preparation Time: 15 minutes | Ready Time: 1 hour 10 minutes

Ingredients:
- 1 3/4 cups all-purpose flour
- 2 teaspoons baking powder
- 1/2 teaspoon salt
- 1/2 cup unsalted butter, softened
- 1/2 cup granulated sugar
- 1/4 cup light brown sugar
- 2 large eggs
- 1 teaspoon vanilla extract
- 1/4 cup warm coffee
- 1 teaspoon instant coffee powder
- 1 cups semisweet chocolate chips

Instructions:
1. Preheat oven to 350F. Grease a 9x5-inch loaf pan.
2. In a medium bowl, sift together the flour, baking powder and salt.
3. In a large bowl, using a hand mixer, beat together the butter, granulated sugar and brown sugar on medium-high speed until light and fluffy (about 3 minutes).
4. Beat in the eggs, one at a time, followed by the vanilla extract, coffee and coffee powder until just combined.
5. With the mixer on low speed, slowly add the dry ingredients and stir until just combined.
6. Fold in the chocolate chips.
7. Pour batter into the prepared pan and bake for 45-55 minutes or until a toothpick inserted in the center comes out clean.
8. Allow to cool completely before slicing.

Nutrition Information:
Per serving (1/8 of the loaf) - 268 calories, 13.5g fat, 35g carbohydrate, 2.5g protein, 2g fiber

91. Hazelnut Bread

Hazelnut Bread is an irresistibly delicious and flavorful loaf of bread toped with sweet, creamy, hazelnuts that adds an extra crunchy texture. Perfect for any meal or snack, Hazelnut Bread is sure to please!

Serving: 4 | Preparation Time: 20 minutes | Ready Time: 50 minutes

Ingredients:
- 2 cups all-purpose flour
- 1/2 tsp salt
- 1/2 tsp cinnamon
- 2 tsp baking powder
- 2 cups hazelnuts
- 1 1/2 cups light brown sugar
- 3/4 cup vegetable oil
- 2 eggs, beaten
- 1/3 cup milk

Instructions:
1. Preheat oven to 350 degrees.
2. Grease and flour a 9x5 inch loaf pan.
3. In a medium bowl, mix together the flour, salt, cinnamon, and baking powder.
4. In another bowl, blend the hazelnuts, brown sugar, oil, eggs, and milk.
5. Add the wet ingredients to the dry ingredients and stir until just moistened.
6. Pour batter into the prepared pan.
7. Bake for 55 minutes or until a toothpick inserted in middle comes out clean.
8. Cool before cutting and serving.

Nutrition Information:
Serving size: 1 Slice

Calories: 204, Total Fat: 12g, Saturated Fat: 1.6g, Unsaturated Fat: 10.4g, Cholesterol: 18mg, Sodium: 90mg, Carbohydrates: 20g, Fiber: 1.2g, Sugar: 9.6g, Protein: 4.4g

92. Apricot Bread

Apricot Bread is an easy yet delicious recipe perfect for a quick breakfast or snack. It is moist and flavorful, loaded with chunks of apricot and a hint of nutmeg. This delicious sweet treat is sure to tantalize taste buds.

Serving: 10-12 pieces | Preparation Time: 20 minutes | Ready Time: 1 hour

Ingredients:
- 2 cups all-purpose flour
- 3/4 teaspoon baking powder
- 1/2 teaspoon baking soda
-1/2 cup sugar
- 2 tablespoons butter, melted
- 2 eggs, slightly beaten
- 1 teaspoon grated nutmeg
- 3/4 cup apricots, diced
- 1/2 cup sour cream

Instruction:
1. Preheat oven to 350F, grease and flour an 8x4 inch loaf pan.
2. In a medium bowl, combine flour, baking powder and baking soda.
3. In a separate large bowl, beat together sugar, melted butter, eggs, nutmeg and sour cream until combined.
4. Add the flour mixture to the wet ingredients and mix until just combined.
5. Fold in apricots.
6. Pour batter into prepared loaf pan and bake for 50 minutes. Test with a toothpick, remove from oven when done.
7. Allow to cool before slicing.

Nutrition Information:

Per 1 serving (1 slice): Calories: 140, Fat: 4.7g, Carbohydrates: 21.2g, Protein: 2.8g

93. Banana Chocolate Swirl Bread

Banana Chocolate Swirl Bread is a sweet and tasty snack that's full of flavour but still healthy. This decadent treat is perfect as a dessert or as a special snack. Featuring a swirl of melted chocolate and a dusting of sugar, this is a treat that will leave you wanting more!

Serving: 10-12 slices | Preparation Time: 20 minutes | Ready Time: 60 minutes

Ingredients:
-3-4 ripe bananas
-3/4 cup vegetable oil
-1 1/2 cups sugar
-2 large eggs
-1 tsp vanilla extract
-2 cups all-purpose flour
-1 teaspoon baking soda
-1 teaspoon baking powder
-1/2 teaspoon salt
-4 ounces semi-sweet chocolate
-1 tablespoon sugar

Instructions:
1. Preheat the oven to 350F. Grease and flour a 9x5-inch loaf pan.
2. In a large bowl, mash the ripe bananas.
3. Add the vegetable oil, sugar, eggs, and vanilla extract, and mix to combine.
4. In a separate bowl, whisk together the flour, baking soda, baking powder, and salt.
5. Add the dry ingredients to the wet ingredients, and mix to combine.
6. Pour the batter into the prepared loaf pan.
7. Melt the chocolate in the microwave and drizzle it over the top of the batter. Swirl it into the batter with a knife.
8. Sprinkle the top with the tablespoon of sugar.

9. Bake for 50-60 minutes, or until a toothpick comes out clean.
10. Allow the loaf to cool before slicing.

Nutrition Information:
Each slice of Banana Chocolate Swirl Bread contains about 120 calories, 5 g of fat, 18 g of carbs, 1 g of protein.

94. Chocolate Peanut Butter Banana Bread

This delicious and comforting Chocolate Peanut Butter Banana Bread is the perfect sweet treat. It's a decadent combination of chocolate, peanut butter, and banana that will satisfy your sweet tooth. The bread is easy to prepare, making it a great choice for busy days.

Serving: 8-10 | Preparation Time: 10 minutes | Ready Time: 1 hour 20 minutes

Ingredients:
- 2 cups all-purpose flour
- 1 teaspoon baking powder
- 1/2 teaspoon baking soda
- 1/2 teaspoon salt
- 1 cup mashed banana
- 1/2 cup peanut butter
- 1/2 cup butter (or coconut oil)
- 3/4 cup light brown sugar
- 1 teaspoon vanilla extract
- 2 large eggs
- 1/4 cup cocoa powder

Instructions:
1. Preheat oven to 350F and lightly grease a standard-sized loaf pan.
2. In a large bowl, mix together the flour, baking powder, baking soda, and salt.
3. In a separate bowl, beat together the banana, peanut butter, butter (or coconut oil) light brown sugar, and vanilla extract until combined.
4. Add the eggs one at a time, mixing well after each addition.

5. Pour the wet ingredients into the dry ingredients, adding the cocoa powder slowly while stirring.
6. Pour the batter into the prepared pan and bake for 1 hour and 20 minutes or until a knife inserted in the center of the loaf comes out clean.
7. Let cool before slicing and serving.

Nutrition Information:
488 calories, 18.5 grams fat, 64.9 grams carbohydrates, and 8.4 grams protein.

95. Sweet Potato Pecan Bread

Sweet Potato Pecan Bread is a delicious and moist quick bread with a hint of sweetness and crunchy pecan pieces. Filled with crushed sweet potatoes, raisins, cinnamon, nutmeg and brown sugar, this delicious treat is sure to be a crowd-pleaser.

Serving: 8-10 | Preparation Time: 25 minutes | Ready Time: 1 hour

Ingredients:
- 1 cup all-purpose flour
- 1 teaspoon baking powder
- 1 teaspoon baking soda
- 1/2 teaspoon salt
- 1 teaspoon cinnamon
- 1/2 teaspoon nutmeg
- 2 cups mashed sweet potato
- 1/2 cup butter, melted
- 1/2 cup light brown sugar
- 2 large eggs, lightly beaten
- 1 teaspoon vanilla extract
- 1/2 cup raisins
- 1/2 cup chopped pecans

Instructions:

1. Preheat oven to 350° F (180°C). Securely line a 9-inch (23 cm) loaf pan with parchment paper.
2. In a medium bowl, whisk together flour, baking powder, baking soda, salt, cinnamon and nutmeg.
3. In a large bowl, mix together mashed sweet potatoes, butter, sugar, eggs, and vanilla extract until combined.
4. Fold in dry ingredients just until all ingredients are combined (be careful not to overmix, you want this batter to be thick and just barely combined).
5. Fold in raisins and pecans.
6. Pour batter into prepared loaf pan and spread evenly with an offset spatula.
7. Bake for 50-60 minutes or until a toothpick inserted into the center comes out clean.
8. Let cool completely before slicing.

Nutrition Information:
Per 1-slice serving: 246 calories, 12.1 g fat, 2.9 g saturated fat, 24.2 g carbohydrates, 1.5 g fiber, 2.4 g protein, 45 mg cholesterol.

96. Cranberry Coconut Bread

This Cranberry Coconut Bread is deliciously moist, sweet and full of tart cranberries and crunchy coconut flakes. Perfect for breakfast or a snack, and so easy to make!

Serving: Makes 1 loaf | Preparation Time: 10 minutes | Ready Time: 60 minutes

Ingredients:
- 1/2 cup maple syrup
- 1 tsp vanilla extract
- 2 eggs
- 1/4 cup melted coconut oil
- 1/4 cup coconut cream
- 1 cup coconut flour
- 1/2 tsp baking powder
- 1/2 tsp baking soda

- 1/2 tsp salt
- 1/2 cup unsweetened coconut flakes
- 1/2 cup dried cranberries

Instructions:
1. Preheat your oven to 350F (175°C). Grease and line a loaf pan with parchment paper.
2. In a medium bowl, whisk together the maple syrup, vanilla extract, eggs, melted coconut oil and coconut cream.
3. In a separate bowl, add the coconut flour, baking powder, baking soda and salt together, and then combine this with the wet ingredients.
4. Stir in the coconut flakes and cranberries until evenly dispersed.
5. Pour the batter into the prepared pan and spread out evenly. Bake for 50-60 minutes or until a toothpick comes out clean.

Nutrition Information:
Calories: 267, Fat: 15.3g, Carbohydrates: 28.5g, Protein: 5.1g, Fiber: 3.6g, Sugar: 12.3g

CONCLUSION

Cooking can be a very rewarding experience. Whether you're a beginner or an experienced cook, 96 Quick Breads: Delicious Recipes for Every Occasion has something for everyone. From sweet- and savory breakfast breads to special-occasion breads and breads perfect for sharing, this cookbook contains delicious recipes for almost every occasion.

Each recipe is easy to follow and comes with step-by-step instructions, as well as helpful tips and tricks to ensure that you get the most out of every helping. Mealtime has never been easier or more enjoyable, as each bread recipe can be prepared in as little as 25 minutes or less. Be sure to use quality ingredients to ensure that your creation turns out just right.

No matter what type of bread you're looking to bake, 96 Quick Breads: Delicious Recipes for Every Occasion has something for you. Whether you're looking for a sweet treat or a savory snack, this cookbook has recipes that will satisfy everyone's taste buds. Get baking and enjoy the fruits of your labor!

Made in the USA
Columbia, SC
17 December 2024

49447730R00061